a little taste of...

italy

a little taste of...

italy

Recipes by Sophie Braimbridge
and Jo Glynn
Photography by Chris L. Jones
Additional text by Kay Halsey

MURDOCH
BOOKS

contents

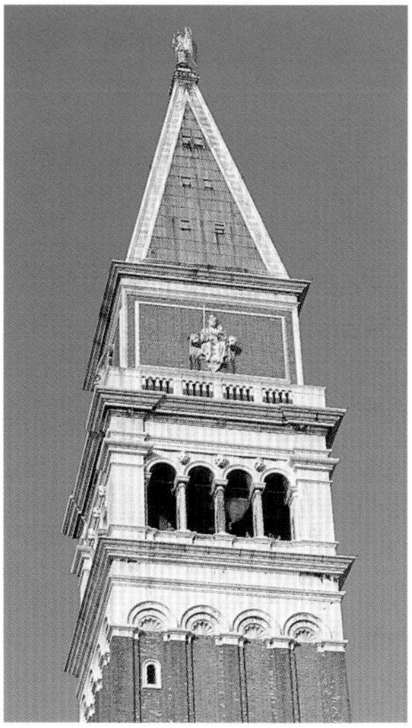

SPECIAL FEATURES

a little taste...

The food of Italy is so good because it is so loved by the Italians themselves. Central to Italy's fabled *dolce vita*, the good life, it is celebrated with family recipes and noisy gatherings; a glass of red wine and some local olives; and *pranzo*, lunch, three or four courses in the neighbourhood restaurant, the clattering and laughter breaking out into the quiet lunchtime streets. The food in these places is not about constant innovation, but constancy. Italians like to eat their local dishes, much-loved recipes tied to the landscape they grew up in, and the result is a real continuity with the past, where women still roll out fresh pasta for lunch and tiny *trattorie* flourish, serving regional specialities to a buzz of workers and families.

There has never been just one Italy but many, and climate, geography and a complex history meant no national style of cooking could ever hope to evolve. In the Italy of the past, this led to a country divided along food lines. The people of the South enjoyed pasta, olive oil and recipes made from their sweet vegetables and fruit. In the North, rice and polenta were the staples, while rich pastures meant an abundance of meat and dairy products. Each region had its own way of doing things and the result was an incredible array of local salami, ham, pasta, oil, cheese and wine.

Of course, the food of Italy has not stood still. As the country changed from a rural to an industrial society, people travelled and food production

became big business, the ways of the old food calendar—the seasonality of produce, proximity to the sea and fresh fish, or to the land and local produce—were no longer so all-important. However, the Italians, ever nostalgic for the traditional rhythms of life, have clung on to, even revitalized, their *cucina regionale.* Today there is an extraordinary interest in cooking local dishes, as well as a great pride in local products and the artisans who make them.

Stretching from the mountains to the Mediterranean, much of the country's beautiful and varied landscape at first seems unsuited to growing all this food. But the Italians have found gems in every corner of their land. The dense woodlands are home to porcini and prized truffles; while pigs, able to thrive anywhere, have been transformed from the food of the poor into salami and sweet prosciutto. The silver-green olive trees scattering the hillsides of Central Italy produce the world's finest olive oil, and in the South the hot conditions that make crop-growing so difficult produce intense tomatoes and eggplants (aubergines), their flavour concentrated by the hot sun. With these ingredients the cooking of Italy has never really been about formality or rules—instead it celebrates simple country food with its own *cucina casalinga*, home-style cooking.

a little taste of...

Casual and often family-run, the pizzeria may have been born in the South but it is now a much-loved institution, even in Italy's most northern towns. Many serve only their own neighbourhood and these can be the most noisy and boisterous of Italy's eateries, a hot evening seeming to draw out a whole village to eat and talk in the pizzeria's courtyard or over a few outside tables. Pizzerias usually open only at night but the wood-burning oven is lit in the day until so red-hot it can cook a pizza in just a few minutes, blasting the thin, flat dough until it puffs up and slightly chars, while the ingredients just melt together. The more traditional the pizzeria, the fewer pizzas on the menu, with some of Naples' most revered establishments making less than five. There is usually a Margherita, with mozzarella, tomato and fresh basil; a simple Marinara with tomato and oregano; a Formaggio, cheese; and a pizza topped with the day's seafood, perhaps a handful of mussels, clams or squid.

...the pizzeria

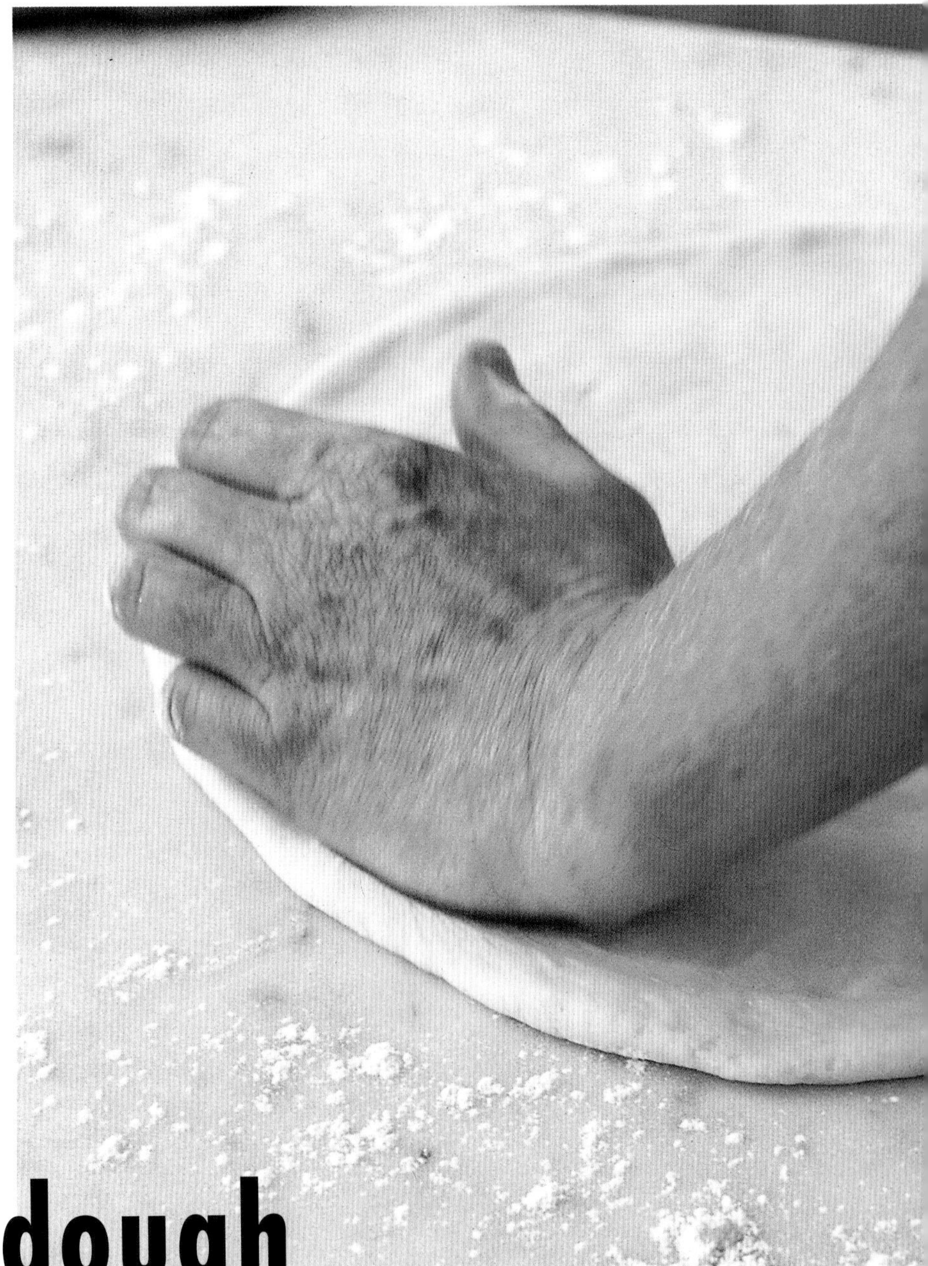

pizza dough

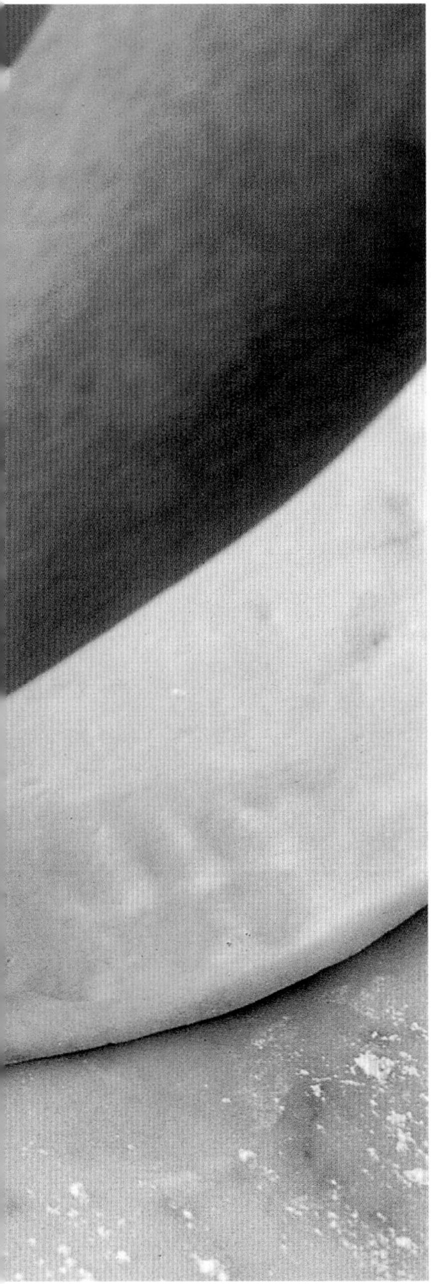

1 tablespoon caster (superfine) sugar
2 teaspoons dried yeast or
15 g (½ oz) fresh yeast
215 ml (7 fl oz) lukewarm water
450 g (3⅔ cups) plain (all-purpose) flour
½ teaspoon salt
3 tablespoons olive oil
cornmeal

Makes two 30 cm (12 inch) pizza bases

Put the sugar and yeast in a small bowl and stir in 90 ml (3 fl oz) of the water. Leave in a draught-free spot to activate. If the yeast does not bubble and foam in 5 minutes, throw it away and start again.

Mix the flour and salt in a bowl or in a food processor fitted with a plastic blade. Add the olive oil, remaining water and the yeast mixture. Mix until the dough loosely clumps together. Transfer to a lightly floured surface and knead for 8 minutes, adding a little flour or a few drops of warm water if necessary, until you have a soft dough that is not sticky but is dry to the touch.

Rub the inside of a large bowl with olive oil. Roll the ball of dough around in the bowl to coat it with oil, then cut a shallow cross on the top of the ball with a sharp knife. Leave the dough in the bowl, cover with a tea towel or put in a plastic bag and leave in a draught-free spot for 1–1½ hours until doubled in size (or leave in the fridge for 8 hours to rise slowly).

Punch down the dough to its original size, then divide into two portions. (At this stage the dough can be stored in the fridge for up to 4 hours, or frozen. Bring back to room temperature before continuing.)

Working with one portion at a time, push the dough out to make a thick circle. Use the heels of your hands and work from the centre of the circle outwards, to flatten the dough into a 30 cm (12 inch) circle with a slightly raised rim. (If you find it difficult to push the dough out by hand you can use a rolling pin.) The pizza dough is now ready to use, as instructed in the recipe. Cook on a lightly oiled tray, dusted with cornmeal, and get it into the oven as quickly as possible.

1 x 30 cm (12 inch) pizza base (page 11)
or 1 bought base
cornmeal
1 quantity tomato sauce (page 251)
150 g (5½ oz) mozzarella cheese, chopped
9 small basil leaves
1 tablespoon olive oil

Makes one pizza

Preheat the oven to 240°C (475°F/Gas 8). Place the pizza base on a baking tray dusted with cornmeal and spoon the tomato sauce onto the base, spreading it up to the rim. Scatter with the mozzarella and basil and drizzle with the oil.

Bake for 12–15 minutes, or until golden and puffed. Remove from the oven and brush the rim with a little extra olive oil before serving.

pizza margherita

calzone

cornmeal
½ quantity pizza dough (page 11) for each calzone
1½ tablespoons olive oil

MOZZARELLA AND PROSCIUTTO
170 g (6 oz) mozzarella cheese, cut into 2 cm (¾ inch) cubes
2 thin slices prosciutto, cut in half
1 artichoke heart, marinated in oil, drained and cut into 3 slices from top to bottom

POTATO, ONION AND SALAMI
2 tablespoons vegetable oil
1 small onion, very thinly sliced
75 g (2½ oz) small red potatoes, unpeeled, very thinly sliced
75 g (2½ oz) mozzarella cheese, chopped
60 g (2¼ oz) sliced salami
2 tablespoons grated Parmesan cheese

Each recipe makes one 25 cm (10 inch) calzone

Preheat the oven to 230°C (450°F/Gas 8). Lightly oil a baking tray and dust with cornmeal.

On a lightly floured surface roll out the dough into an 18 cm (7 inch) circle. Now, using the heels of your hands and working from the centre outwards, press the circle out to a diameter of about 30 cm (12 inch). Transfer to the baking tray. Brush the entire surface lightly with the oil.

To make the mozzarella and prosciutto calzone, spread the mozzarella cheese over one half of the pizza base, leaving a narrow border around the edge. Roll the half slices of prosciutto into little tubes and place on top of the cheese. Top with the artichoke slices, then season well.

To make the potato, onion and salami calzone, heat the oil in a frying pan and add the onion slices. Cook for 1 minute, then scatter the potato on top. Cook, stirring, for 3–4 minutes, until beginning to brown. Season with salt and pepper. Spread over one half of the pizza base, leaving a narrow border around the edge. Scatter the mozzarella on top, followed by the salami slices and Parmesan.

Whichever calzone you are making, now fold the plain side of the base over the filling to make a half-moon shape. Match the cut edges and press them firmly together to seal. Fold them over and press into a scrolled pattern to thoroughly seal in the filling. Brush the surface with a little extra olive oil, then transfer to the oven. Bake for about 20 minutes, until the crust is golden.

pizza & panini... It's no surprise that the food-loving Italians refuse to restrict themselves to just three meals a day. To do so would be to deny themselves one of life's great pleasures—fast-food, Italian-style. Pizza slices topped with crushed *pomodori* and basil; warm panini sandwiches eaten standing at the bar; salty, rosemary-spiked focaccia—Italy's flat bread; and hot spit-roasted chicken from the *rosticceria.*

Once all these were regarded as mere snacks, a little something to keep you going until the midday meal. But food on the go is now lunch in the international cities of Italy, from Milan in the North to Naples in the South, and the most popular lunch of all is *pizza al taglio.* Invented in Rome, these rectangular slices of thin, crispy pizza can be bought in bakeries and *pizzerie* all over Italy. In the capital itself, the best are found in tiny holes-in-the-wall. Made fresh on the premises, just two or three pizzas are out on the counter at any one time, with a rotation of toppings drawn from a chalked-up board of the day's combinations. A line of hungry customers waits to see what will be pulled next from the wood-fired oven—choosing from a simple *funghi* or *rucola* (rocket) to a *pizza bianca,* with its wonderful steaming aroma from

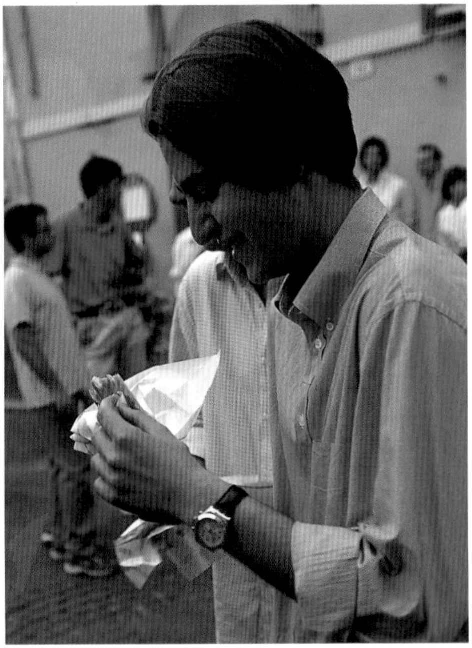

the charcoal-hot pizza and its simple topping of olive oil, rosemary and garlic. Sold by weight, a portion is cut to size to be eaten in the nearest piazza.

Italian bars and *paninoteca* provide tempting alternatives to pizza. Panini are the classic Italian sandwiches, while *tramezzini* are the almost old-fashioned version—crustless white sandwiches, cut on the diagonal into perfect triangles. Combinations are plain but delicious—a local salami or prosciutto with a chunk of cheese or a few slices of tomato. Crushed in the sandwich press, they make a melting lunch, wrapped in greaseproof paper to go. The marketplace is another source of food on the run, with stalls set up early to feed both stallholders and customers. It is here you might find *porchetta*—possibly Italy's first fast food—a whole roast suckling pig carved to order into rolls and sold hot from the proprietor's tiny van.

1 x 30 cm (12 inch) pizza base (page 11) or 1 bought base
cornmeal
1 quantity tomato sauce (page 251)
1 tablespoon grated Parmesan cheese
60 g (2¼ oz) mozzarella cheese, chopped
30 g (1 oz) thinly sliced prosciutto, cut into small pieces
1 Roma (plum) tomato, thinly sliced
3 basil leaves, shredded
4 small artichoke hearts, marinated in oil, drained and quartered
4 button mushrooms, sliced
pinch of dried oregano
1 tablespoon olive oil

Makes one pizza

Preheat the oven to 240°C (475°F/Gas 8). Place the pizza base on a baking tray dusted with cornmeal and spoon the tomato sauce onto the base, spreading it up to the rim. Sprinkle the Parmesan on top.

Visually divide the pizza into quarters. Scatter the mozzarella over two opposite quarters. Spread the prosciutto over one of these and arrange the tomato over the other. Lightly salt the tomato and sprinkle on the basil.

Arrange the artichoke over the third quarter and the mushrooms over the final quarter. Sprinkle the oregano over both these sections. Drizzle the oil over the pizza. Bake for 12–15 minutes, or until golden and puffed.

pizza quattro stagioni

pizzette

½ quantity pizza dough (page 11)
cornmeal
1 tablespoon olive oil
250 g (9 oz) mozzarella cheese, grated

GARLIC AND ROSEMARY PIZZETTE
4 garlic cloves, crushed
2 teaspoons chopped rosemary
1½ tablespoons olive oil
50 g (½ cup) grated Parmesan cheese
3 garlic cloves, thinly sliced

TOMATO AND OLIVE PIZZETTE
200 g (7 oz) pitted black olives, diced
400 g (14 oz) Roma (plum) tomatoes, diced
3 garlic cloves, crushed
2 tablespoons finely shredded basil
3 tablespoons olive oil
5 small sprigs of basil

Makes 10 pizzette

Preheat the oven to 240°C (475°C/Gas 8). Form the pizza dough into ten bases. Place the pizza bases on two baking trays dusted with cornmeal. Brush with the oil, then sprinkle the bases with mozzarella. Make five garlic and rosemary pizzette and five tomato and olive pizzette.

To make the garlic and rosemary pizzette, scatter five bases with the crushed garlic and rosemary and drizzle the oil over the top. Sprinkle with Parmesan and garnish with some slices of garlic.

To make the tomato and olive pizzette, mix together the olives, tomato, garlic and shredded basil and spoon over the remaining bases. Drizzle over the oil and garnish with the sprigs of basil.

Bake the pizzette for 10 minutes, or until the bases are crisp and golden.

RISTORANTE
DA
NANE MORA
PIZZERIA
GIARDINO
5864
5866

RISTORANTE
DA
NANE MORA
PIZZERIA
GIARDINO
CORTE PRIMA
DEL MILION
O DEL FORNO

2 tablespoons olive oil
2 garlic cloves, crushed
2 tablespoons pine nuts
1 kg (2 lb 4 oz) spinach, roughly chopped
1 x 30 cm (12 inch) pizza base (page 11) or 1 bought base
cornmeal
1 quantity tomato sauce (page 251)
220 g (8 oz) mozzarella cheese, chopped
15 very small black olives, such as Ligurian
3 tablespoons grated Parmesan cheese

Makes one pizza

Preheat the oven to 240°C (475°F/Gas 8). Heat the oil in a frying pan and fry the garlic and pine nuts over low heat until golden. Add the spinach, then increase the heat and stir until wilted. Season.

Place the pizza base on a baking tray dusted with cornmeal and spoon the tomato sauce onto the base, spreading it up to the rim. Sprinkle with half the mozzarella. Spread the spinach and olives over the top, followed by the rest of the mozzarella and the Parmesan.

Bake for 12–15 minutes, or until golden and puffed. Brush the rim with a little extra olive oil before serving.

pizza spinaci

pizza melanzana

220 g (8 oz) long thin eggplants (aubergines), thinly sliced
60 ml (1/4 cup) olive oil
1 x 30 cm (12 inch) pizza base (page 11) or 1 bought base
cornmeal
1 quantity tomato sauce (page 251), with a pinch of chilli flakes added
170 g (6 oz) mozzarella cheese, chopped
15 black olives
1 tablespoon capers
4 tablespoons grated pecorino cheese
1 tablespoon olive oil

Makes one pizza

Layer the eggplant in a colander, sprinkling salt on each layer. Leave to drain for 1 hour. Wipe off the salt with paper towels. Preheat the oven to 240°C (475°F/Gas 8).

Heat the olive oil in a large frying pan and quickly brown the eggplant on both sides, cooking in batches. Drain on paper towels.

Place the pizza base on a baking tray dusted with cornmeal and spoon the tomato sauce onto the base, spreading it up to the rim. Arrange the eggplant in a circular pattern over the top, then scatter with mozzarella. Cover with the olives, capers and pecorino, then drizzle with the oil. Bake for 12–15 minutes, or until golden and puffed.

a little taste of...

In the best of Italy's trattorie, the owner's son or daughter reads out the day's offerings, usually a small repertoire of local dishes, the region's comfort food. Perhaps a plate of mountain salami, a little chargrilled fennel or a home-made pasta to start, followed by a steak grilled over wood embers, a roast or some salt cod, all accompanied by a carafe of the young local red or white wine. While many new trattorie are interchangeable with the traditionally more upmarket restaurants, unfussy and cheap establishments can still be found outside the city centres, serving a loyal neighbourhood who come to socialize as much as to eat. Most of the cooking is done by women, while the service is busy and informal, with families often ordering large plates of the *primi* (starters) or *dolci* (desserts) to share. As the volume level rises, eating gives way to drinking, and meals end with a shot of dark espresso and a *digestivo*, the bottle left on the table to top up glasses as needed.

...trattoria

chargrilled asparagus

24 asparagus spears
1 tablespoon extra virgin olive oil
2 tablespoons balsamic vinegar
Parmesan cheese shavings

Serves 4

Wash the asparagus and remove the woody ends (hold each spear at both ends and bend it gently—it will snap at its natural breaking point).

Put the asparagus in a bowl, add the olive oil and toss well. Heat a chargrill pan (griddle) or barbecue and cook the asparagus for about 10 minutes, or until *al dente*. Drizzle with balsamic vinegar and sprinkle with the Parmesan to serve.

(If you don't have a chargrill pan (griddle) or barbecue, you can steam the asparagus or boil in salted water for 6–8 minutes until *al dente*. Drain and mix with the olive oil, balsamic and Parmesan.)

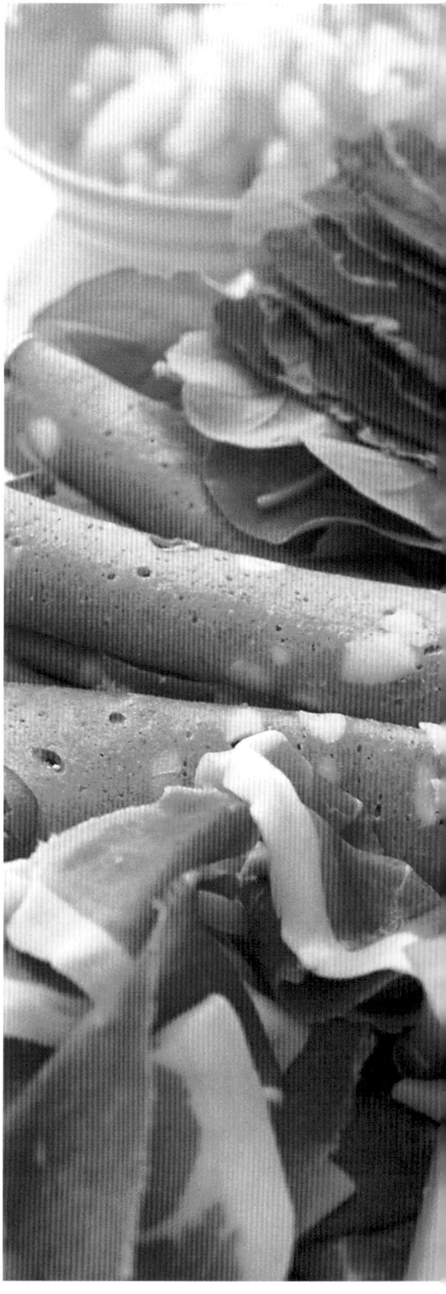

8 slices mortadella
8 slices prosciutto
12 slices coppa
15 slices bresaola (air-dried beef)
15–20 slices casalinga (coarse) salami or finocchiona (Tuscan salami with fennel seeds)
young rocket (arugula) leaves
lemon wedges
extra virgin olive oil
quartered fresh figs or slices of honeydew melon or cantaloupe
cipolline agrodolce (pickled onions)
green olives
cetriolini (small gherkins)
'country-style' bread, such as ciabatta

Serves 6

Arrange the meat around a large platter. Vary the presentation by rolling up the mortadella, for instance, or folding large salami slices into a half-moon shape. Use the rocket as a bed for the coppa or bresaola.

Place the lemon wedges by the prosciutto and drizzle extra virgin olive oil over the bresaola. Arrange the figs or slices of melon next to the prosciutto.

Serve the onions, olives and cetriolini separately in bowls, and provide plenty of sliced bread. Also have on hand the bottle of extra virgin olive oil and plenty of black pepper.

affettati misti

bagna caôda

40 pieces assorted raw vegetables (carrot, celery, fennel or cauliflower florets)
185 ml (3/4 cup) olive oil
6 garlic cloves, crushed
120 g (4 1/2 oz) anchovy fillets, finely minced
90 g (3 1/4 oz) butter
'country-style' bread, such as ciabatta

Serves 4

Trim, wash and dry the vegetables and cut them into strips for dipping.

Put the oil, garlic and anchovies in a saucepan and place it over moderately low heat. Cook gently, stirring once or twice, until the anchovies dissolve. Do not let the garlic brown. Add the butter and leave over low heat until it has melted. Season with pepper.

Transfer the sauce to a bowl and keep it warm at the table by placing on a food warmer or over a burner or spirit stove. Serve the vegetables and bread arranged on a platter. Guests dip their choice of vegetable into the bagna caôda and use a piece of bread to catch any stray drips.

antipasto

The very idea of antipasto sums up Italy's relationship with food. Meaning 'to eat before a meal', it can translate to just a few salt-cured olives or some slices of local salami—something to whet the appetite. But it can also mean so much more—a course of its own—from the bright vegetarian antipasti of the South to plates of wafer-thin bresaola in the North. Sometimes the antipasto seems to almost serve the purpose of prolonging the meal, the pre-course to maybe three or four more dishes, and a little sample of a region's best produce. In the South, this is intense, sun-ripened vegetables—capsicums (peppers), zucchini (courgettes) and eggplants (aubergines)—brushed with a little local olive oil and grilled. In Rome, *carciofini* (young artichokes) and zucchini (courgette) flowers come into season in the spring and are eaten as part of a plate of *fritto misto*, fried in a whispy light batter. Piemonte is home to Italy's greatest tradition of antipasto, and their *bagna caôda* is a dip of warm olive oil and anchovies served in the winter, while in Venice, *antipasto di frutti di mare* is the grandest of all—the freshest seafood from the lagoon dressed simply with lemon juice and olive oil.

4 long thin eggplants (aubergines)
4 zucchini (courgettes)
4 Roma (plum) tomatoes
1 small red capsicum (pepper)
1 small green capsicum (pepper)
1 small yellow capsicum (pepper)
60 ml (¼ cup) olive oil
2 garlic cloves, halved

DRESSING
60 ml (¼ cup) extra virgin olive oil
1 tablespoon balsamic vinegar
1 garlic clove, crushed
3 tablespoons chopped parsley
¼ teaspoon caster (superfine) sugar

Serves 4

Slice the eggplants and zucchini diagonally into 1 cm (½ inch) thick pieces. Halve the tomatoes lengthways and slice the capsicums into short strips. Place all the vegetables in a bowl and add the olive oil and the garlic. Toss well.

Heat a chargrill pan (griddle) or barbecue and brush with oil. Cook the eggplant and zucchini for 2–4 minutes on each side, or until browned. Transfer to a shallow serving dish. Cook the tomatoes and capsicum for 1–2 minutes on each side, or until the capsicum starts to smell sweet and their skins blister. Transfer to the serving dish and set aside to cool.

To make the dressing, mix together all the ingredients and then season. Drizzle the dressing over the vegetables and toss lightly. Serve the salad at room temperature.

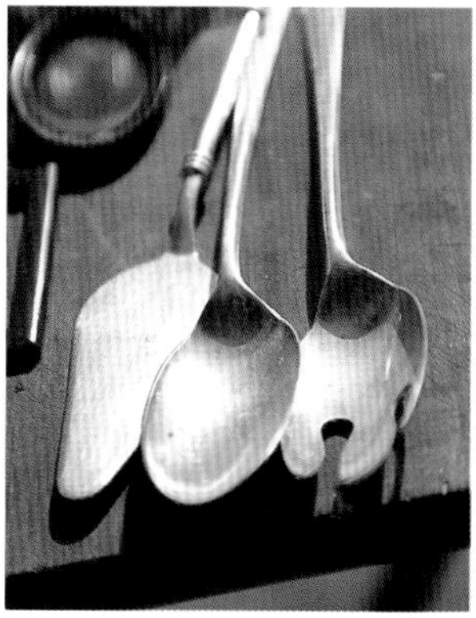

chargrilled vegetable salad

mushroom risotto

20 g (1 oz) dried porcini mushrooms
1 litre (4 cups) vegetable or chicken stock
2 tablespoons olive oil
1 tablespoon butter
1 small onion, finely chopped
2 garlic cloves, crushed
375 g (1¾ cups) risotto rice (arborio, vialone nano or carnaroli)
250 g (9 oz) mushrooms, sliced
pinch of ground nutmeg
50 g (½ cup) grated Parmesan cheese
3 tablespoons finely chopped parsley

Serves 4

Soak the porcini in 500 ml (2 cups) boiling water for 30 minutes. Drain, retaining the liquid. Chop the porcini mushrooms and pass the liquid through a fine sieve. Put the stock in a saucepan, bring to the boil and then maintain at a low simmer.

Heat the olive oil and butter in a large wide heavy-based saucepan. Cook the onion and garlic until softened but not browned. Add the rice and reduce the heat to low. Season and stir briefly to thoroughly coat the rice. Toss in the fresh mushrooms and nutmeg. Season and cook, stirring, for 1–2 minutes. Add the porcini and their liquid, increase the heat and cook until the liquid has been absorbed.

Stir in a ladleful of stock and cook over moderate heat, stirring continuously. When the stock has been absorbed, stir in another ladleful. Continue like this for about 20 minutes, until all the stock has been added and the rice is *al dente*. (You may not need to use all the stock, or you may need a little extra.) Remove from the heat and stir in the Parmesan and parsley. Season and serve.

45 g (1½ oz) unsalted butter, melted
30 g (⅓ cup) grated Parmesan cheese
3 egg yolks
1 litre (4 cups) milk
pinch of ground nutmeg
200 g (1⅔ cups) semolina flour

TOPPING
40 g (1½ oz) butter, melted
80 ml (⅓ cup) thick (double) cream
35 g (⅓ cup) grated Parmesan cheese

Serves 4

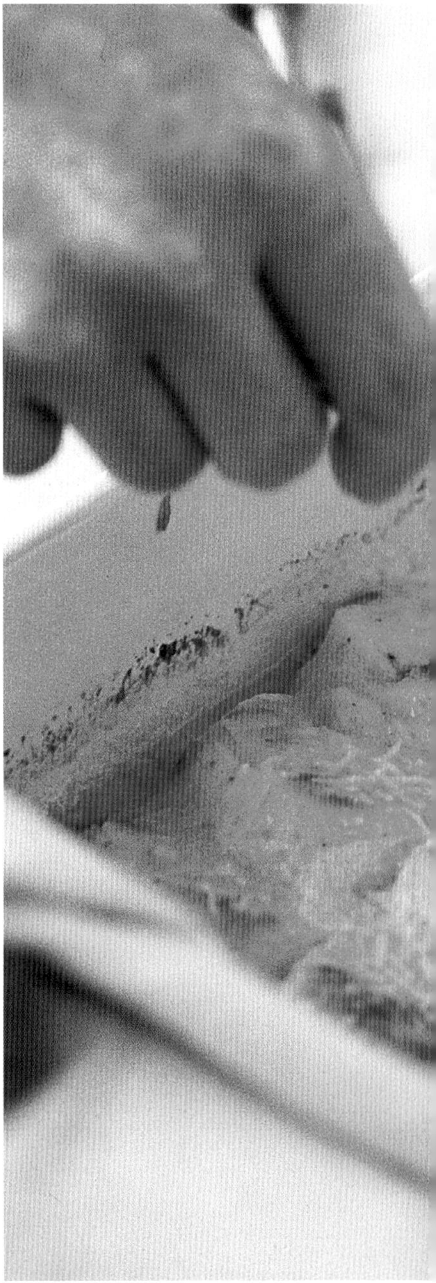

Line a 30 x 25 cm (12 x 10 inch) swiss roll tin with baking paper. Beat together the butter, Parmesan and egg yolks and season lightly. Set aside.

Heat the milk in a large saucepan. Add the nutmeg, and season with salt and pepper. When the milk is just boiling, pour in the semolina in a steady stream, stirring as you pour. Reduce the heat and continue to cook, stirring, for about 10–12 minutes, or until all the milk has been absorbed and the mixture pulls away from the side of the pan in one mass.

Remove the pan from the heat and beat in the egg yolk mixture. When smooth, spoon quickly into the swiss roll tin. Smooth the surface to give an even thickness, using a knife dipped in cold water. Set aside to cool.

Preheat the oven to 180°C (350°F/Gas 4) and grease a 25 x 18 cm (10 x 7 inch) shallow casserole or baking tray.

Lift the semolina slab out of the tin and peel off the baking paper. Cut the semolina into circles, using a 4 cm (1½ inch) biscuit cutter dipped in cold water. Arrange the circles, slightly overlapping, in the greased casserole.

To make the topping, blend together the butter and cream. Pour this over the gnocchi and sprinkle the Parmesan on top. Transfer to the oven and bake for about 25–30 minutes, or until golden. Serve at once.

roman gnocchi

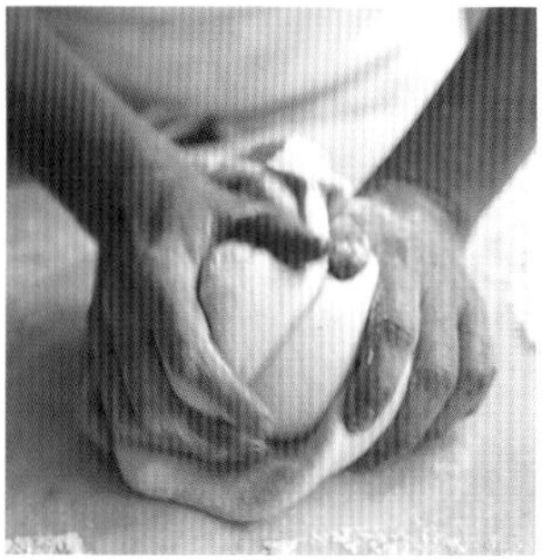

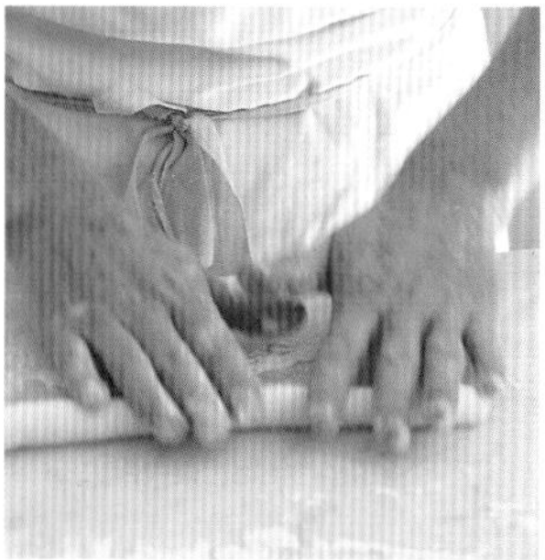

potato gnocchi with pancetta

GNOCCHI
1 kg (2 lb 4 oz) floury potatoes, unpeeled
2 egg yolks
2 tablespoons grated Parmesan cheese
125–185 g (1–1½ cups) plain (all-purpose) flour

SAUCE
1 tablespoon butter
75 g (2½ oz) pancetta or bacon, cut into thin strips
8 very small sage or basil leaves
125 ml (½ cup) thick (double) cream
50 g (½ cup) grated Parmesan cheese

Serves 4

Prick the potatoes all over, then bake for 1 hour, or until tender. Leave to cool for 15 minutes, then peel and mash, or put through a ricer or a food mill (do not use a blender or food processor).

Mix in the egg yolks and Parmesan, then gradually stir in the flour. When the mixture gets too dry to use a spoon, work with your hands. Once a loose dough forms, transfer to a lightly floured surface and knead gently. Work in enough extra flour to give a soft, pliable dough that is damp to the touch but not sticky.

Divide the dough into six portions. Working with one portion at a time, roll out on the floured surface to make a rope about 1.5 cm (⅝ inch) thick. Cut the rope into 1.5 cm (⅝ inch) lengths. Take one piece of dough and press your finger into it to form a concave shape, then roll the outer surface over the tines of a fork to make deep ridges. Fold the outer lips in towards each other to make a hollow in the middle. Continue with the remaining dough.

Bring a large saucepan of salted water to the boil. Add the gnocchi in batches, about 20 at a time. Stir gently and return to the boil. Cook for 1–2 minutes, or until they rise to the surface. Remove them with a slotted spoon, drain and put in a greased shallow casserole or baking tray. Preheat the oven to 200°C (400°F/Gas 6).

To make the sauce, melt the butter in a small frying pan and fry the pancetta strips until crisp. Stir in the sage leaves and cream. Season and simmer for 10 minutes, or until thickened. Pour the sauce over the gnocchi, toss gently and sprinkle the Parmesan on top. Bake for 10–15 minutes, or until the Parmesan melts and turns golden. Serve hot.

400 g (14 oz) spaghetti
2 eggs
2 egg yolks
65 g (2/3 cup) grated Parmesan cheese, plus extra for serving
2 tablespoons olive oil
30 g (1 oz) butter
2 garlic cloves
200 g (7 oz) pancetta, cut into small strips

Serves 4

Cook the spaghetti in a large saucepan of boiling salted water until *al dente*. Meanwhile, mix the eggs, egg yolks and Parmesan together in a bowl and season lightly.

Heat the oil and butter in a large frying pan. Bruise the garlic cloves with the back of a knife and add to the pan with the pancetta. Cook over moderate heat until the pancetta is crisp, discarding the garlic when it becomes golden.

Drain the spaghetti, add to the frying pan and toss well. Remove from the heat and stir in the egg mixture. Serve immediately, with Parmesan.

spaghetti carbonara

TUGNOLI

spaghetti vongole

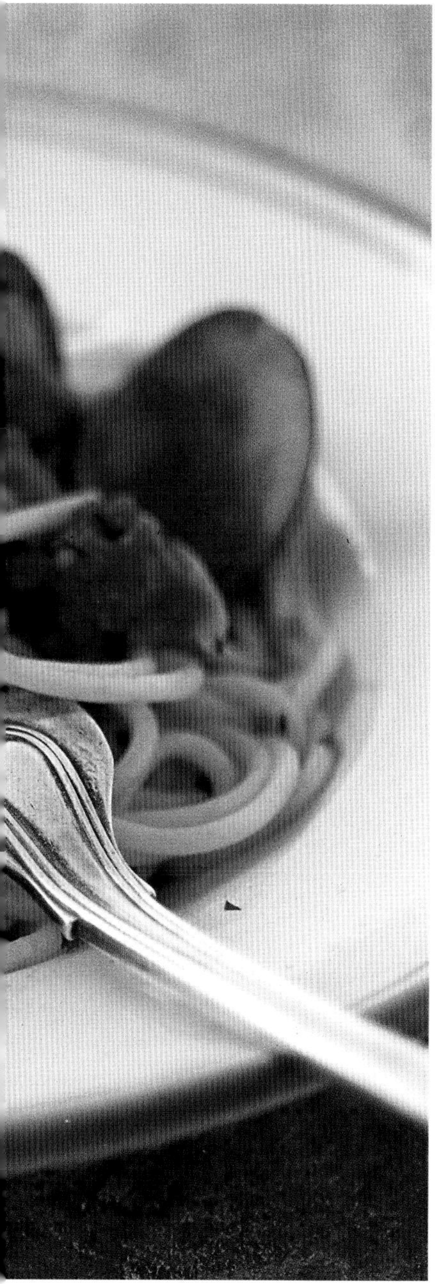

2 tablespoons olive oil
3 garlic cloves, crushed
2 pinches of chilli flakes
1 teaspoon chopped parsley
125 ml (½ cup) dry white wine
2 x 400 g (14 oz) tins chopped tomatoes
1 kg (2 lb 4 oz) clams (vongole)
3 tablespoons finely chopped parsley
400 g (14 oz) spaghetti or linguine
½ teaspoon grated lemon zest
lemon wedges

Serves 4

Heat the oil in a large deep frying pan. Add the garlic and chilli and cook over low heat for 30 seconds. Add the chopped parsley, wine and tomato. Increase the heat and boil, stirring occasionally, for 8–10 minutes, until the liquid is reduced by half.

Clean the clams by scrubbing them thoroughly. Rinse well under running water. Discard any that are broken or cracked or do not close when tapped on the work surface. Add to the saucepan. Cover the pan, increase the heat and cook for 3–5 minutes until the clams open. Shake the pan often. Remove the clams from the pan, discarding any that stay closed. Stir in the finely chopped parsley and season. Uncover the pan and boil until thick. Set 12 clams aside and extract the meat from the rest.

Cook the pasta in a large saucepan of boiling salted water until *al dente*. Drain and stir through the sauce. Add the lemon zest, reserved clams and clam meat and toss well. Serve with the lemon wedges.

2 tablespoons olive oil
2 large garlic cloves, thinly sliced
1–2 medium-sized dried chillies
2 x 400 g (14 oz) tins tomatoes
400 g (14 oz) penne or rigatoni
1 sprig of basil, torn into pieces

Serves 4

Heat the olive oil in a saucepan and add the garlic and chillies. Cook over low heat until the garlic is light golden brown. Turn the chillies over during cooking so both sides get a chance to infuse in the oil and turn slightly nutty in flavour. Add the tomatoes and season with salt. Cook gently, breaking up the tomatoes with a wooden spoon, for about 20–30 minutes, or until the sauce is rich and thick.

Meanwhile, cook the pasta in a large saucepan of boiling salted water until *al dente*. Drain.

Add the basil to the sauce and season just before serving. Toss the sauce with the pasta. If you prefer a hotter sauce, break open the chilli to release the seeds.

penne all'arrabbiata

bucatini all'amatriciana

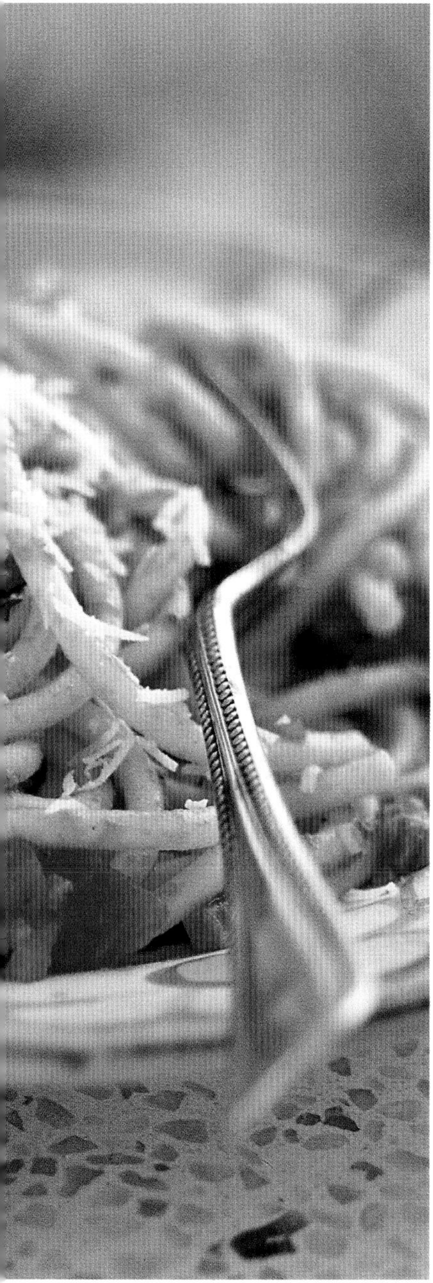

1 tablespoon olive oil
150 g (5½ oz) guanciale or pancetta, in 2 thick slices
1 small onion, finely chopped
2 garlic cloves, crushed
¾ teaspoon dried chilli flakes
600 g (1 lb 5 oz) tinned chopped tomatoes
400 g (14 oz) bucatini
2 tablespoons finely chopped parsley
grated Parmesan cheese

Serves 4

Heat the oil in a large saucepan. Trim the rind and fat from the pancetta and add them to the pan. Cook over medium-high heat until the fat is crisp, to extract the liquid fat, then discard the crispy fat and rinds. Dice the pancetta, add to the liquid fat in the saucepan and cook until lightly browned.

Add the onion and fry gently for about 6 minutes, or until soft. Add the garlic and the chilli flakes and cook, stirring, for 15–20 seconds, then stir in the tomato. Season with salt and pepper.

Simmer the sauce for about 15 minutes, or until it thickens and darkens.

Meanwhile, cook the bucatini in a large saucepan of boiling salted water until *al dente*. Stir the parsley into the sauce, drain the pasta, toss together well and serve with Parmesan.

FILLING
900 g (2 lb) pumpkin or butternut squash, peeled and cubed
6 tablespoons olive oil
1 small red onion, finely chopped
90 g (1/3 cup) ricotta cheese
1 egg yolk, beaten
25 g (1/4 cup) grated Parmesan cheese
1 teaspoon grated nutmeg
2 tablespoons chopped sage

1 packet fresh lasagne sheets
1 egg
2 teaspoons milk

SAGE BUTTER
250 g (9 oz) butter
10 g (1/2 cup) sage leaves

grated Parmesan cheese

Serves 6

To make the filling, preheat the oven to 190°C (375°F/Gas 5). Put the pumpkin in a roasting tin with half the olive oil and lots of salt and pepper. Bake in the oven for 40 minutes, or until it is completely soft.

Meanwhile, heat the remaining oil in a saucepan and gently cook the onion until soft. Put the onion and pumpkin in a bowl, draining off any excess oil. Mash, leave to cool, then crumble in the ricotta. Mix in the egg yolk, Parmesan, nutmeg and sage. Season well.

To make the tortellini, cut the lasagne sheets into 8 cm (3 inch) squares. Mix together the egg and milk to make an egg wash and brush lightly over the pasta just before you fill each one. Put a small teaspoon of filling in the middle of each square and fold it over diagonally to make a triangle, pressing down the corners. Pinch together the two corners on the longer side. (If you are not using the tortellini immediately, place them, well spaced out, on baking paper dusted with cornmeal and cover with a tea towel. They can be left for 1–2 hours before cooking—don't refrigerate or they will become damp.)

Cook the tortellini, in small batches, in a large saucepan of boiling salted water until *al dente*. Remove and drain with a slotted spoon.

To make the sage butter, melt the butter slowly with the sage and leave to infuse for at least 5 minutes. Drizzle over the tortellini and serve with a sprinkling of Parmesan.

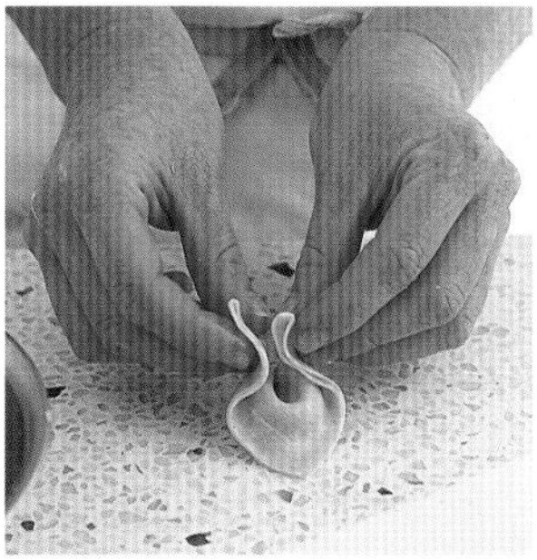

tortellini filled with pumpkin and sage

cannelloni

MEAT SAUCE
3 tablespoons olive oil
1 onion, finely chopped
2 garlic cloves, crushed
120 g (4½ oz) bacon, finely chopped
60 g (2¼ oz) button mushrooms, finely chopped
¼ teaspoon dried basil
220 g (8 oz) minced (ground) pork
220 g (8 oz) minced (ground) veal
1 tablespoon finely chopped parsley
200 g (7 oz) tin chopped tomatoes
250 ml (1 cup) beef stock
3 tablespoons dried breadcrumbs
1 egg

10 sheets fresh lasagne, about 17 x 12 cm/7 x 5 inches (the grain of the pasta should run with the width not the length, or the pasta will split when rolled up)
3 x quantity tomato sauce (page 251)
4 large slices prosciutto, cut in half
60 g (½ cup) grated fontina cheese
185 ml (¾ cup) thick (double) cream
65 g (⅔ cup) grated Parmesan cheese

Serves 4

To make the meat sauce, heat the oil in a frying pan and cook the onion, garlic and bacon over moderate heat for 6 minutes, or until the onion is soft and golden. Stir in the mushrooms and basil, cook for 2–3 minutes, then add the pork and veal. Cook, stirring often to break up the lumps, until the mince has changed colour. Season well, add the parsley, tomato and stock, partially cover the pan and simmer for 1 hour. Remove the lid and simmer for another 30 minutes to reduce the liquid. Cool slightly, then stir in the breadcrumbs, then the egg.

Cook the lasagne sheets in batches in a large saucepan of boiling salted water until *al dente*. Scoop out each batch and drain.

Preheat the oven to 190°C (375°F/Gas 5). Grease a shallow 30 x 18 cm (12 x 7 inch) ovenproof dish and spoon the tomato sauce over the base.

Place a half slice of prosciutto over each pasta sheet. Top with a sprinkling of fontina. Spoon an eighth of the meat filling across one end of the pasta sheet. Starting from this end, roll the pasta up tightly to enclose the filling. Place the filled rolls, seam side down, in a row in the dish.

Beat together the cream and Parmesan and season well. Spoon over the cannelloni so that it is covered. Bake for 20 minutes, or until lightly browned on top. Leave to rest for 10 minutes before serving.

tagliatelle & tortellini… Is it pasta that truly united Italy? Once the division between the affluent North and rural South was drawn on the Italian dinner plate—the rich risotto, polenta and fresh egg pasta of the North against the lean spaghetti and *pomodori* of the South—and all this food symbolized with its ties to the land that grew it. But now a love of the pasta of the South seems to have taken in not only much of the world, but the entire Italian population as well.

The eating of pasta in Italy has a special touch of its own that is rarely found elsewhere. Almost always the *primo piatto* rather than the main event, the way pasta should be eaten is something for which the Italians have a natural instinct. Just undercooked to retain an *al dente*, or biting, texture,

shapes are carefully matched with their sauces. Wide, flat tagliatelle are paired with cream; spaghetti with thick ragùs that cling to the strands; and cup-shaped orecchiette perfectly hold their traditional sauce of broccoli or turnip tops.

Dried pasta was born in Naples and it was in this dynamic city that one of the great food combinations was created—threads of pasta with a sauce made from the ripest tomatoes, grown in the rich volcanic soil of the city's dangerous neighbour—Mount Vesuvius. This simple sauce reflects the way Italians like to treat their pasta. Never meant to be more than a starting point for a meal, it usually comes with just a coating of sauce—perhaps a spoonful of cooking juices from the meat course; flakes of chilli and some olive oil; or melted butter and leaves of sage. Only in the main-course soups and stews of rural Italy does pasta play a bigger role, providing sustenance to dishes such as *pasta e fagioli,* pasta and beans.

In the North, the love is of fresh pasta, especially the tiny parcels of tortellini, anolini and cappellacci stuffed with pork, pumpkin, herbs or soft, fresh cheese. Made from the region's soft wheat, the pasta is bought fresh daily or made and rolled out by hand at home, and treated with little fuss, slipped into a clear *brodo* or covered with butter or herbs.

200 g (7 oz) squid tubes
4 tablespoons olive oil
1 onion, finely chopped
1 celery stalk, finely chopped
1 carrot, finely chopped
2 garlic cloves, finely chopped
15 g (1/4 cup) roughly chopped parsley
pinch of cayenne pepper
1 fennel bulb, trimmed and thinly sliced
125 ml (1/2 cup) dry white wine
400 g (14 oz) tin chopped tomatoes
1.5 litres (6 cups) fish stock (page 250)
300 g (10 1/2 oz) fish fillets, such as red mullet, monkfish, cod, deep sea perch
250 g (9 oz) scallops, cleaned
12 prawns (shrimp)

CROSTINI
3 tablespoons extra virgin olive oil
2 garlic cloves, crushed
4 slices 'country-style' bread, such as ciabatta

Serves 4

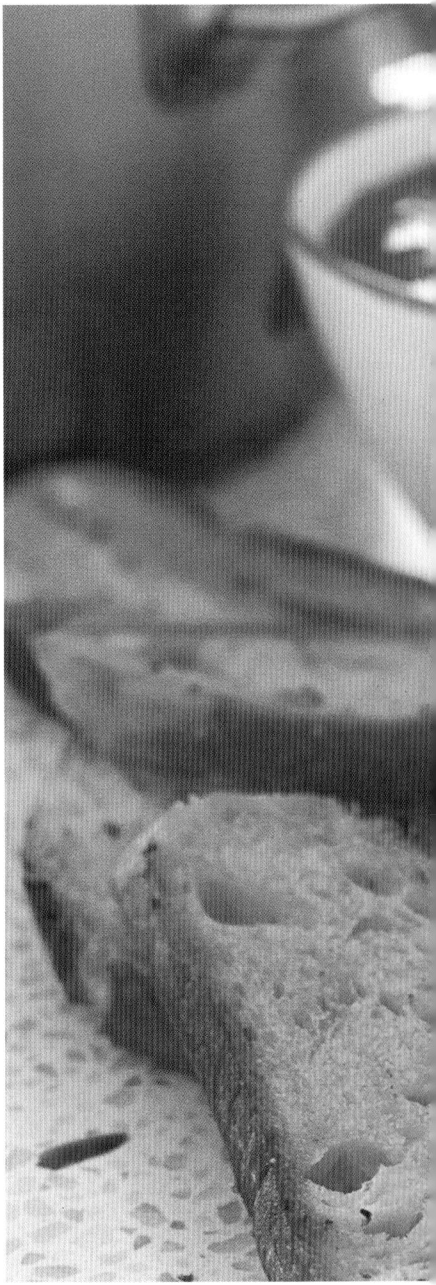

Place the squid out flat, with the skin side up, and score a crisscross pattern into the flesh, being careful not to cut all the way through. Slice diagonally into bite-sized strips.

Heat the oil in a large saucepan and cook the onion, celery, carrot, garlic and chopped parsley over moderately low heat for 5–6 minutes, or until softened but not browned. Add the cayenne pepper and season well. Stir in the fennel and cook for 2–3 minutes. Add the white wine, increase the heat and cook until it has been absorbed. Stir in the tomatoes, then add the fish stock and bring to the boil. Reduce the heat and simmer for 20 minutes.

Add the squid to the pan with the fish pieces and simmer for 1 minute. Add the scallops and prawns and simmer for another 2 minutes. Taste and add more seasoning if necessary.

To make the crostini, heat the olive oil and crushed garlic in a large frying pan over moderately low heat. Add the slices of bread and fry on both sides until golden. Place a slice of bread into each of four warmed serving bowls. Ladle the soup on top and serve immediately.

zuppa di pesce

stuffed mussels

24 mussels
3 tablespoons olive oil
4 garlic cloves, crushed
500 ml (2 cups) tomato passata
1½ tablespoons roughly chopped basil
15 g (¼ cup) finely chopped parsley
40 g (½ cup) fresh white breadcrumbs
2 eggs, beaten
pinch of cayenne pepper

Serves 4

Clean the mussels by scrubbing them thoroughly. Discard any that are broken or cracked or do not close when tapped on the work surface. Insert a sharp knife at the point where the beard protrudes and prise the shell open, leaving the mussel intact inside and keeping the two shells attached. Pull out the beard and discard. Rinse the mussels.

Heat the oil in a large saucepan and gently cook half the garlic for 15–20 seconds, without browning. Add the passata and basil, season lightly with salt and pepper and bring to the boil. Reduce the heat and simmer for 5 minutes, then add 315 ml (1¼ cups) cold water. Return to the boil, then cover and keep at a low simmer until needed.

Combine the parsley, breadcrumbs and the remaining garlic, then blend in the eggs. Add the cayenne pepper and season. Using a teaspoon, fill each mussel with a little of this mixture. Tie the mussels closed with kitchen string as you go, to prevent the filling escaping.

When the mussels have all been stuffed, place them in the tomato sauce and simmer, covered, for 10 minutes.

Lift out the mussels with a slotted spoon and remove the string. Pile on a warm platter and serve with the tomato sauce, bread and finger bowls.

2 x 900 g (2 lb) chickens
170 ml (2/3 cup) olive oil
juice of 1 large lemon
2 sage leaves
3–4 very small red chillies, finely minced, or 1/2 teaspoon dried chilli flakes
2 French shallots
2 garlic cloves
4 tablespoons chopped parsley
2 1/2 tablespoons softened butter
lemon slices or wedges

Serves 4

Split each chicken through the breastbone and press open to form a butterfly, joined down the back. Flatten with your hand to give a uniform surface for cooking. Place in a shallow dish large enough to take both chickens side by side.

Mix together the olive oil, lemon juice, sage and chilli in a bowl and season well with salt and pepper. Pour over the chicken and leave to marinate in the fridge for 30 minutes. Turn the chickens and leave for another 30 minutes.

Meanwhile, chop the shallots, garlic, parsley and butter in a blender or food processor until fine and paste-like. (If you want to do this by hand, chop the vegetables and then mix them into the softened butter.) Season with salt and pepper. Preheat the grill (broiler).

Place the chickens, skin side down, on a grill (broiler) tray. Position about 10 cm (4 inches) below the heat and grill (broil) for 10 minutes, basting with the marinade once or twice. Turn the chickens and grill (broil), basting occasionally, for another 10–12 minutes, or until the juices run clear when a thigh is pierced deeply with a skewer.

Spread the butter paste over the skin of the chickens with a knife. Reduce the heat and grill (broil) for about 3 minutes until the coating is lightly browned. Serve hot or cold, with lemon slices or wedges.

pollo alla diavola

veal alla milanese

8 veal chops
2 eggs
50 g (½ cup) fine dried breadcrumbs
3 tablespoons grated Parmesan cheese
3 tablespoons butter
1 tablespoon oil
4 lemon wedges dipped in finely chopped parsley

Serves 4

Cut all the fat from the veal chops and trim the lower rib bone until it is clean of all fat and flesh. Place each chop between two sheets of plastic wrap and pound the flesh with a meat mallet until it is half its original thickness.

Lightly beat the eggs with salt and pepper and pour into a dish. Combine the breadcrumbs and Parmesan and place in another dish. Dip each chop into the egg, coating it on both sides. Shake off the excess egg, then coat the chop with the breadcrumb mix, pressing each side firmly into the crumbs. Place all the chops on a plate and chill for 30 minutes.

Heat the butter and oil in a large frying pan. As soon as the butter stops foaming, add the chops and fry gently for 4 minutes on each side, until the breadcrumbs are deep golden. Serve immediately with the lemon wedges.

30

4 rib or rump steaks
4 tablespoons olive oil
550 g (1 lb 4 oz) tomatoes
3 garlic cloves, crushed
3 basil leaves, torn into pieces
1 teaspoon finely chopped parsley

Serves 4

Brush the steaks with 1 tablespoon of the olive oil and season well. Put the steaks on a plate and set aside.

Score a cross in the top of each tomato. Plunge the tomatoes into boiling water for 20 seconds, then drain and peel the skin away from the cross. Chop the tomatoes, discarding the cores.

Heat 2 tablespoons of the olive oil in a saucepan over low heat and add the garlic. Soften without browning for 1–2 minutes, then add the tomato and season. Increase the heat, bring to the boil and cook for 5 minutes. Stir in the basil.

Heat the remaining oil in a large frying pan with a tight-fitting lid. Brown the steaks over moderately high heat for 2 minutes on each side (cook in batches rather than overcrowding the pan). Place in a slightly overlapping row down the centre of the pan and spoon the sauce over the top, covering the steaks completely. Cover the pan and cook over low heat for about 5 minutes, or until the steaks are cooked to your taste. Sprinkle the parsley over the top and serve at once.

bistecca alla pizzaiola

sausage and lentil stew

3 tablespoons olive oil
850 g (1 lb 14 oz) Italian sausages
1 onion, chopped
3 garlic cloves, thinly sliced
1½ tablespoons chopped rosemary
2 x 400 g (14 oz) tins chopped tomatoes
16 juniper berries, lightly crushed
pinch of grated nutmeg
1 bay leaf
1 dried chilli, crushed
185 ml (¾ cup) red wine
95 g (½ cup) green lentils

Serves 4

Heat the oil in a large saucepan and cook the sausages for 5–10 minutes, until browned. Remove the sausages from the pan and reduce the heat. Add the onion and garlic to the pan and cook gently until the onion is soft.

Stir in the rosemary, then add the tomato and cook gently until reduced to a thick sauce. Add the juniper berries, nutmeg, bay leaf, chilli, wine and 410 ml (1⅔ cups) water. Bring to the boil, then add the lentils and sausages. Give the stew a good stir, cover the pan and simmer gently for about 40 minutes, or until the lentils are soft. Stir a couple of times to prevent the lentils sticking to the base of the pan. Add a little more water if the lentils are still not cooked.

2 tablespoons olive oil
60 g (2¼ oz) butter
2 large onions, halved and thinly sliced
600 g (1 lb 5 oz) calves liver, very thinly sliced
1 tablespoon finely chopped parsley
lemon wedges

Serves 4

Heat the olive oil and half the butter in a large frying pan and add the onion. Cover and cook over low heat for 30–40 minutes, stirring from time to time, until very soft and golden. Season well with salt and pepper and transfer to a bowl.

Melt the remaining butter in the frying pan, increase the heat and fry the liver quickly until brown on all sides. Return the onion to the pan and cook, stirring often, for 1–2 minutes more, or until the liver is cooked. Remove from the heat, stir in the parsley and check for seasoning. Serve with lemon wedges.

venetian liver

grilled tomatoes

4 large ripe tomatoes
2 garlic cloves, crushed
60 ml (1/4 cup) olive oil
1 tablespoon chopped parsley

Serves 4

Cut the tomatoes in half horizontally. Place the tomato halves on a baking tray, with the skin side up, then grill (broil) them for 2 minutes before turning them over. Mix together the garlic, olive oil and parsley and drizzle over the tomatoes. Season with salt and pepper.

Put the tomatoes back under the grill (broiler) and cook for 6 minutes, or until cooked. Serve hot or warm.

80 ml (1/3 cup) extra virgin olive oil
750 g (1 lb 10 oz) floury potatoes, cut into 4 cm (1 1/2 inch) cubes
long sprig of rosemary
sea salt

Serves 4

Preheat the oven to 170°C (325°F/Gas 3). Pour the oil into a shallow casserole or baking tray. Toss the potato into the casserole, turning to coat thoroughly in oil, then spread out so that the pieces aren't touching. Scatter the rosemary leaves over the potatoes.

Roast for 30 minutes, then turn and sprinkle generously with sea salt. Return to the oven and roast for another 30–40 minutes, or until crisp and golden. Serve hot or cold.

roasted rosemary potatoes

a little taste of...

Thought of as upmarket, with waiters and tablecloths, service and sommeliers—the Italian restaurant can be smart and serious, but it can also be a family-run establishment, where excellence in the kitchen, simple or refined, runs through to knowledge and style front-of-house. Only in a restaurant can you really sample innovative Italian cooking or food from outside the region, as well as choose wine from an extensive list. The best chefs will cook according to the produce in the markets, and dishes not on the menu might include the new season's porcini or *carciofi* (artichokes) or a special filled pasta. Meals begin with antipasto, perhaps fried baby squid or zucchini (courgette) flowers, followed by a *primo* of soup, pasta or risotto. The *secondo* of meat or fish is usually quite plain, chargrilled and served simply with a wedge of lemon, while the *contorni* is a portion of whatever is in season, from thin green beans to crushed *fagioli* drizzled with olive oil. The list of *dolci* (desserts) is rarely extensive, with many Italians choosing some *frutta* (fruit), a gelato or just a little cheese.

...restaurant

warm artichokes vinaigrette

4 x 350 g (12 oz) artichokes
juice of 1 lemon

VINAIGRETTE
2 tablespoons lemon juice
4 tablespoons olive oil
2 teaspoons finely chopped onion or 1 finely chopped shallot
1 tablespoon chopped parsley

Serves 4

Bring a large pan of salted water to the boil. Cut off the artichoke stalks at the base so the artichokes stand upright. Put them in the boiling water and add the lemon juice. Boil gently for 30–40 minutes, or until a leaf from the base comes away easily. Cool quickly under cold running water and drain upside down on a tray.

Combine all the ingredients for the vinaigrette by whisking in a bowl or putting them in a tightly sealed screwtop jar and shaking well. Season with salt and pepper.

To serve, put each artichoke on a serving plate and gently prise it open a little. Spoon the vinaigrette over the top, letting it drizzle into the artichoke and around the plate.

(To eat the artichokes, scrape off the flesh from the leaves between your teeth, then remove and discard the furry choke at the base with a spoon. You can now eat the tender base or 'heart'.)

700 g (1 lb 9 oz) good-quality beef fillet
1 egg yolk
3 teaspoons Dijon mustard
3 tablespoons lemon juice
2 drops Tabasco sauce
60 ml (1/4 cup) olive oil
1 tablespoon cream
2–3 tablespoons capers, rinsed

Serves 6

Put the beef in the freezer for half an hour, or until it is firm. Using a sharp knife or mandolin, cut the beef into paper-thin slices. Cover six serving plates with the beef in an even layer.

Blend together the egg yolk, mustard, lemon juice and Tabasco sauce in a bowl or food processor. Add the olive oil in a thin stream, whisking or processing continuously until the mayonnaise thickens. Whisk in the cream. Season to taste with salt and pepper, then drizzle over the beef slices and sprinkle with capers.

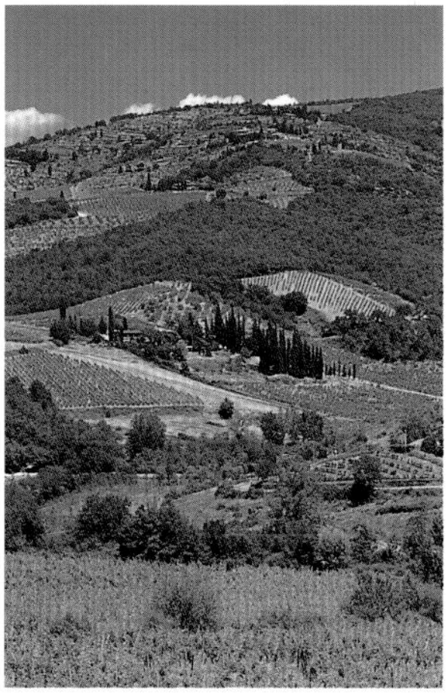

carpaccio

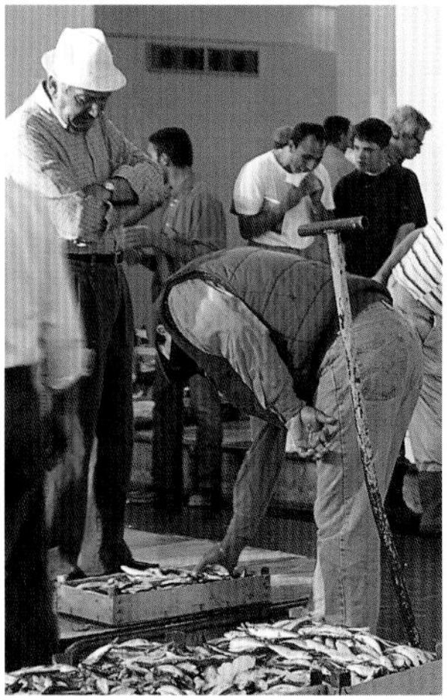

fritto misto di mare

250 g (9 oz) baby squid
12 large prawns (shrimp)
8 small octopus
16 scallops, cleaned
12 fresh sardines, gutted and heads removed
250 g (9 oz) firm white fish fillets (such as ling, cod or snapper), skinned and cut into large cubes

GARLIC AND ANCHOVY SAUCE
125 ml (½ cup) extra virgin olive oil
2 garlic cloves, crushed
3 anchovy fillets, finely minced
2 tablespoons finely chopped parsley
pinch of chilli flakes

BATTER
200 g (1⅔ cups) plain (all-purpose) flour
80 ml (⅓ cup) olive oil
1 large egg white

oil for deep-frying
lemon wedges

Serves 4

Preheat the oven to 140°C (275°F/Gas 1). Clean the squid by pulling the heads and tentacles out of the bodies along with any innards. Cut the heads off below the eyes, just leaving the tentacles. Discard the heads and set the tentacles aside. Rinse the bodies, pulling out the clear quills, and cut the bodies into rings. Peel and devein the prawns, leaving the tails intact. Clean the octopus by slitting the head and pulling out the innards. Cut out the eyes and hard beak and rinse. If the octopus are big, halve or quarter them.

To make the sauce, warm the oil in a frying pan. Add the garlic, anchovy, parsley and chilli flakes. Cook over low heat for 1 minute, or until the garlic is soft but not brown. Serve warm or chilled.

To make the batter, sift the flour into a bowl and stir in ¼ teaspoon salt. Mix in the oil with a wooden spoon, then gradually add 315 ml (1¼ cups) tepid water, changing to a whisk when the mixture becomes liquid. Whisk until the batter is smooth and thick. Stiffly whisk the egg white and fold into the batter. Heat the oil in a deep-fat fryer or deep frying pan to 190°C (375°F), or until a piece of bread fries golden brown in 10 seconds when dropped in the oil.

Dry the seafood on paper towels so the batter will stick. Working with one type of seafood at a time, dip the pieces in batter. Shake off the excess batter, then carefully lower into the oil. Deep-fry for 2–3 minutes, depending on the size of the pieces. Drain on paper towels, then transfer to the oven. Do not crowd the seafood. Keep warm while you fry the remaining seafood. Serve immediately with lemon wedges and the sauce.

6 ripe Roma (plum) tomatoes
3–4 balls mozzarella cheese
2 tablespoons extra virgin olive oil
15 young basil leaves
½ teaspoon balsamic vinegar (optional)

Serves 4

Slice the tomatoes, pouring off any excess juice, and cut the mozzarella into slices of a similar thickness.

Arrange alternating rows of tomato and mozzarella on a serving plate. Sprinkle with salt and pepper and drizzle the olive oil over the top. Tear the basil leaves into pieces and scatter over the oil. To serve, take to the table and sprinkle with the balsamic vinegar, if you're using it.

insalata caprese

milanese risotto

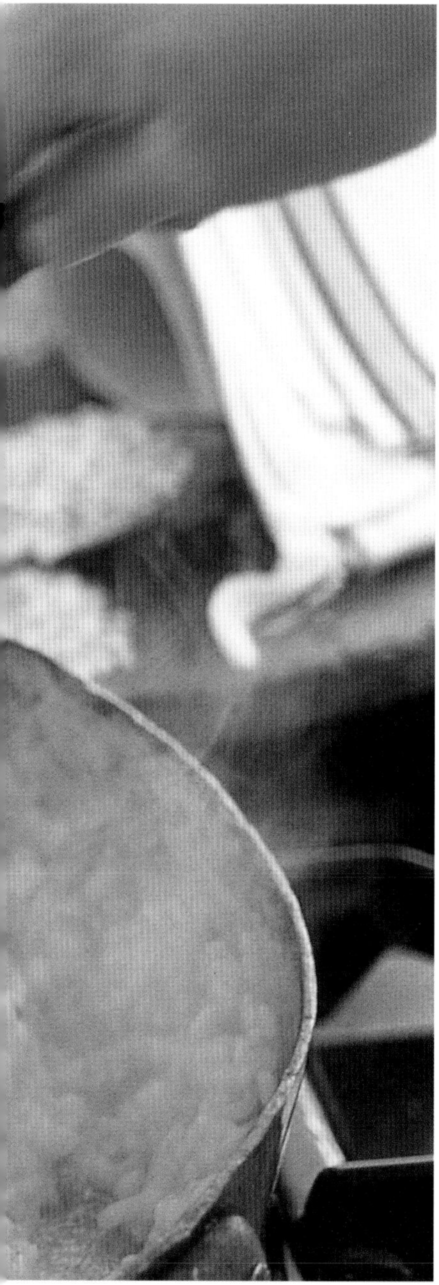

185 ml (3/4 cup) dry white vermouth or white wine
large pinch of saffron threads
1.5 litres (6 cups) chicken stock
100 g (3 1/2 oz) butter
75 g (2 1/2 oz) beef marrow
1 large onion, finely chopped
1 garlic clove, crushed
360 g (1 2/3 cups) risotto rice (arborio, vialone nano or carnaroli)
50 g (1/2 cup) grated Parmesan cheese

Serves 6 as a side dish

Put the vermouth in a bowl, add the saffron and leave to soak. Put the stock in a saucepan, bring to the boil and then maintain at a low simmer.

Melt the butter and beef marrow in a large wide heavy-based saucepan. Add the onion and garlic and cook until softened but not browned. Add the rice and reduce the heat to low. Season and stir briefly to thoroughly coat the rice.

Add the vermouth and saffron to the rice. Increase the heat and cook, stirring, until all the liquid has been absorbed. Stir in a ladleful of the simmering stock and cook over moderate heat, stirring continuously. When the stock has been absorbed, stir in another ladleful. Continue like this for about 20 minutes, until all the stock has been added and the rice is *al dente*. (You may not need to use all the stock, or you may need a little extra—every risotto will be slightly different.)

Stir in a handful of Parmesan and serve the rest on the side for people to help themselves.

formaggi… Italy produces hundreds of wonderful *formaggi,* many unavailable outside the country, but perhaps just two best articulate Italy's diverse cheese-making traditions—the noble, aged *Parmigiano reggiano* of the North and the soft, fresh *mozzarella di bufala* of the South.

Undoubtedly the king of Italy's *formaggi,* the great *Parmigiano reggiano* is made with true reverence and to strict regulations in the rich, northern pastures of Parma and Reggio Emilia. This cheese is the true Parmesan, the only one of Italy's many *grana,* or hard, grating cheeses, entitled to use the name—found proudly branded onto each rind.

Each wheel of cheese is made from around 500 litres of milk, whose curds are scooped up in a length of cloth and later left to mature in vast 'cathedrals'. The best is kept for as long as 3 to 4 years, until very hard and dark and it forms the perfect grating cheese. Never cut, the wheels are cracked open by forcing small knives into the rind, then carved into crumbling, uneven portions.

Parmesan is integral to the cooking of the North, where it is combined with other treasures of that countryside—sweet *Prosciutto di Parma, porcini*, butter and cream—to make one of many sauces for the local tortellini or polenta. Its distinctive taste is uniquely Italian, and the strong flavour is almost always allowed to shine through—freshly grated over oven-roasted vegetables, added to a simple risotto or served with a piece of pear. Thought of only as a cooking cheese outside of Italy, in the towns of Emilia-Romagna it is also eaten as a table cheese, its grainy texture partnered with sweet fresh figs or paper-thin slices of the region's Parma ham.

Mozzarella di bufala is part of a tradition of soft cheeses from the South. Usually now made with cow's milk, *fior di latte*, only in a few places can you still find mozzarella made from the milk of buffaloes, and in most of these cases the producers are family cheese-makers, who look after their herd and make the cheese following traditional farming rhythms. Made fresh each morning, the curds are shaped into balls under boiling water by the master cheese-maker, each one uniquely formed by the shape of his hands. Around Naples it can be found served unadorned—a pure white ball, sometimes still warm—to be eaten as a simple antipasto, with a drizzle of olive oil, some salt and black pepper. When cut open, the cheese is so fresh it falls meltingly away, uncovering its soft centre and a pool of milky whey.

175 g (6 oz) squid tubes
200 g (7 oz) prawns (shrimp)
4 tablespoons olive oil
2 garlic cloves, crushed
175 g (6 oz) firm white fish fillets, such as monkfish, sea bass or fresh haddock, skinned and cut into bite-sized pieces
16 scallops, cleaned
1 litre (4 cups) fish stock (page 250)
1 leek, white part only, thinly sliced
360 g (1⅔ cups) risotto rice (arborio, vialone nano or carnaroli)
125 ml (½ cup) dry white wine
3 Roma (plum) tomatoes, chopped
1 tablespoon butter
1½ tablespoons finely chopped parsley
1½ tablespoons finely chopped dill

Serves 4

Cut the squid tubes into thinner rings. Peel and devein the prawns.

Heat half the olive oil in a large wide heavy-based saucepan. Add the garlic and cook gently without browning for 20–30 seconds. Add the squid and prawns and season lightly. Increase the heat and cook until they turn opaque. Remove the squid and prawns from the pan and set aside.

Add the fish and scallops to the pan and cook until the fish and scallops change colour. Remove from the pan and set aside.

Put the stock in a saucepan, bring to the boil and then maintain the stock at a low simmer.

Add the remaining olive oil to the large wide pan. Add the leek and cook for 3–4 minutes, or until softened but not browned. Add the rice and reduce the heat to low. Season and stir briefly to coat the rice, then add the white wine. Increase the heat and cook, stirring, until all the liquid has been absorbed.

Stir in a ladleful of the simmering stock and cook over moderate heat, stirring continuously. When the stock has been absorbed, stir in another ladleful. Continue like this for about 20 minutes, until all the stock has been added and the rice is *al dente*. (You may not need to use all the stock, or you may need a little extra—every risotto will be slightly different. If you prefer, add more stock to make the risotto more liquid.) Add the tomato and cooked seafood and toss lightly.

Remove the saucepan from the heat and gently stir in the butter and herbs. Season with salt and black pepper. Spoon into warm bowls and serve.

seafood risotto

red wine risotto

500 ml (2 cups) chicken stock
100 g (3½ oz) butter
1 onion, finely chopped
1 large garlic clove, crushed
2 tablespoons chopped thyme
220 g (1 cup) risotto rice (arborio, vialone nano or carnaroli)
500 ml (2 cups) dry red wine
50 g (½ cup) grated Parmesan cheese

Serves 4 as a starter

Put the chicken stock in a saucepan, bring to the boil and then maintain at a low simmer.

Heat the butter in a large wide heavy-based saucepan. Add the onion and garlic and cook until softened but not browned. Add the thyme and rice and reduce the heat to low. Season and stir briefly to thoroughly coat the rice.

Pour in half the red wine. Increase the heat and cook, stirring, until all the liquid has been absorbed. Stir in a ladleful of the simmering stock and cook over moderate heat, stirring continuously. When the stock has been absorbed, stir in another ladleful. Continue like this for about 10 minutes, until you have added half the stock.

Add the remaining red wine to the risotto, stirring continuously until it has been absorbed. Stir in another ladleful of the stock, then continue for about 10 minutes, until all the stock has been added and the rice is *al dente*. (You may not need to use all the stock, or you may need a little extra as every risotto will be slightly different.)

Stir in half the Parmesan just before serving, with the remaining cheese to be sprinkled on top.

2 medium-sized squid
1 litre (4 cups) fish stock (page 250)
100 g (3½ oz) butter
1 red onion, finely chopped
2 garlic cloves, crushed
360 g (1⅔ cups) risotto rice (arborio, vialone nano or carnaroli)
3 sachets of squid or cuttlefish ink, or the ink sac of a large cuttlefish
175 ml (⅔ cup) white wine
2 teaspoons olive oil

Serves 6 as a starter

Prepare the squid by pulling the heads and tentacles out of the bodies along with any innards. Cut the heads off below the eyes, leaving just the tentacles. Discard the heads and set the tentacles aside. Rinse the bodies, pulling out the transparent quills. Finely chop the bodies.

Pour the fish stock into a saucepan, bring to the boil and then maintain at a low simmer.

Heat the butter in a large wide heavy-based saucepan and cook the onion until softened but not browned. Increase the heat and add the chopped squid. Cook for 3–5 minutes, or until the squid turns opaque. Add the garlic and stir briefly. Add the rice and reduce the heat to low. Season and stir briefly to thoroughly coat the rice.

Squeeze out the ink from the sachets and add to the rice with the wine. Increase the heat and stir until all the liquid has been absorbed.

Stir in a ladleful of the simmering stock and cook over moderate heat, stirring continuously. When the stock has been absorbed, stir in another ladleful. Continue like this for about 20 minutes, until all the stock has been added and the rice is *al dente*. (You may not need to use all the stock, or you may need a little extra—every risotto will be slightly different.)

Heat the olive oil in a frying pan and fry the squid tentacles quickly. Garnish the risotto with the tentacles and serve immediately.

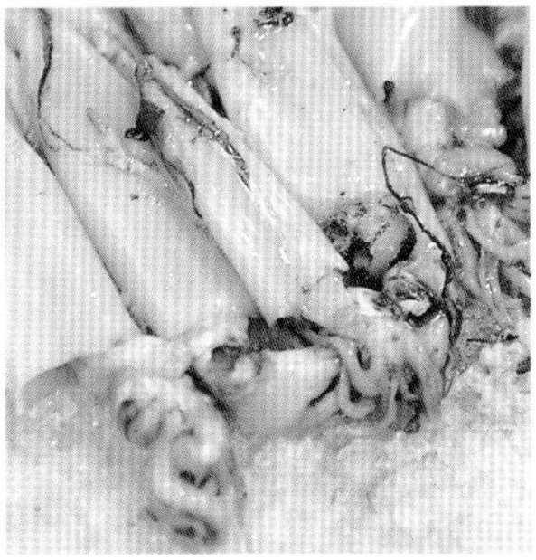

risotto nero

crespelle

CREPES
200 g (1⅔ cups) plain (all-purpose) flour
3 eggs
250 ml (1 cup) milk
3–4 tablespoons butter

HAM, EGG AND ASPARAGUS FILLING
150 g (5½ oz) asparagus, chopped
20 g (1 oz) butter
1 tablespoon plain (all-purpose) flour
125 ml (½ cup) hot milk
2 tablespoons grated Parmesan cheese
1 teaspoon chopped basil
2 eggs, hard-boiled and chopped
120 g (4 oz) ham, cut into strips
50 g (1¾ oz) melted butter, for brushing
75 g (¾ cup) grated Parmesan cheese, for sprinkling

Makes 12 crepes

To make the crepes, put the flour in a bowl, make a well in the centre and add the eggs and a good pinch of salt. Mix well with a wooden spoon. Gradually pour in the milk combined with 185 ml (¾ cup) water, whisking constantly until you have a smooth, runny batter. Leave to rest for 2 hours.

Stir the batter and add a little more water, if necessary, to return it to the original consistency. Heat a little butter in an 18 cm (7 inch) crepe pan. Spoon in 2–3 tablespoons of batter, tilting the pan to cover the base. Cook for 1 minute, until brown but not set, then turn over with a spatula and cook for another 30 seconds until set. Slide onto a plate and cook the rest of the batter. Preheat the oven to 180°C (350°F/Gas 4).

To make the ham, egg and asparagus filling, simmer the asparagus in boiling salted water for 3 minutes. Melt the butter in a saucepan, stir in the flour, then add the hot milk, stirring until you have a thick sauce. Stir in the Parmesan, basil, eggs, asparagus and ham, and season well.

Place a spoonful of filling in the centre of each crepe and roll up, or fold it in half and then half again. Place in a greased shallow ovenproof dish or baking tray, sprinkle the melted butter and Parmesan on top and bake for 20 minutes.

Amedeo

135 g (5 oz) butter
1 garlic clove
400 g (14 oz) fresh tagliatelle
65 g (2/3 cup) grated Parmesan cheese
1 small white Alba truffle or black Norcia truffle

Serves 4 as a starter

Melt the butter in a saucepan over moderately low heat. Add the garlic clove and heat until the butter bubbles, separates and turns lightly golden. Strain the butter.

Meanwhile, cook the pasta in a large saucepan of boiling salted water until *al dente*. Drain and return to the saucepan. Add the browned butter and the Parmesan. Season with salt and black pepper and toss lightly.

Place on warmed plates and take to the table. Using a mandolin or potato peeler, shave a few very thin slices of the truffle onto each serving.

tagliatelle with truffles

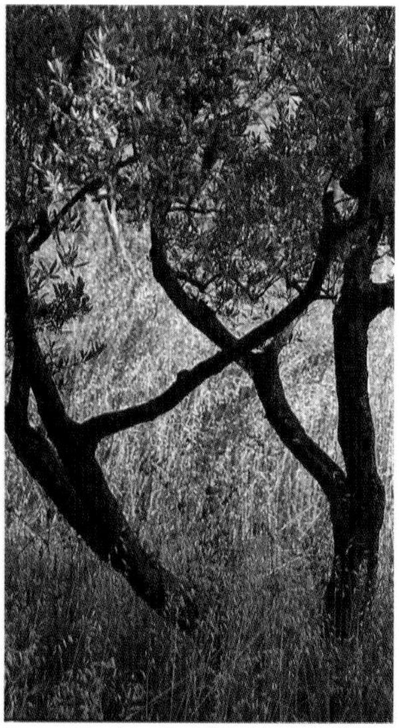

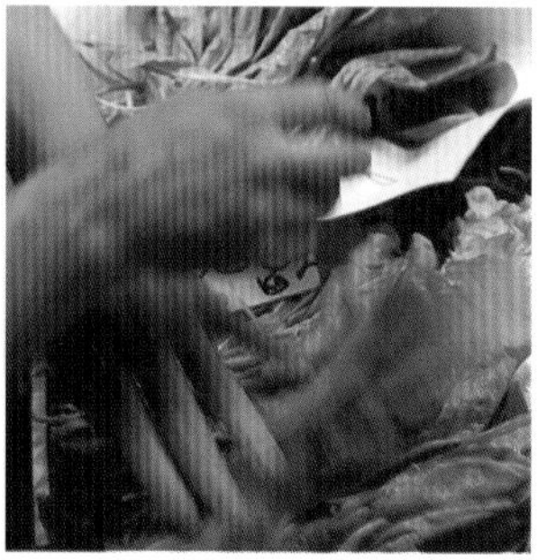

ravioli aperto

FILLING
30 g (1 oz) butter
1 small onion, finely chopped
85 g (3 oz) baby spinach leaves
250 g (1 cup) ricotta cheese
3 tablespoons thick (double) cream

1 packet fresh lasagne sheets
100 g (3½ oz) frozen spinach, thawed
250 ml (1 cup) chicken stock

Serves 4

To make the filling, melt the butter in a frying pan and add the onion. Cook, stirring, for 5 minutes, or until softened. Add the baby spinach leaves and cook for 4 minutes. Remove from the heat and when they are cooled to room temperature, chop them. Add the ricotta and 2 tablespoons of the cream and stir well. Season with salt and pepper.

To make the ravioli, cut the lasagne sheets into sixteen 8 cm (3 inch) squares and cook in a large saucepan of boiling salted water until *al dente*. Drain. Preheat the oven to 180°C (350°F/Gas 4).

Line a baking tray with baking paper and lay out half the pasta squares on the tray. Divide the filling into eight portions and spoon into the centre of each square. Place the other eight pasta squares on top to enclose the filling and cover with a damp tea towel.

To make a sauce, blend the spinach with a little of the chicken stock until smooth. Transfer to a saucepan with the remaining stock and heat for 2 minutes. Add the remaining cream, stir well, season and remove from the heat.

Heat the ravioli in the oven for 5 minutes, or until just warm. Place two ravioli on each plate, reheat the sauce gently, pour over the ravioli and serve immediately.

16 small octopus (about 1.5 kg/3 lb 5 oz)
175 ml (2/3 cup) extra virgin olive oil
4 sprigs of thyme
2 bay leaves
2 garlic cloves, crushed
lemon wedges

Serves 4

Clean the octopus by slitting the head and pulling out the innards. Cut out the eyes and hard beak and rinse. Skin the octopus tentacles and make small diagonal cuts along their length, cutting about a third of the way through the tentacle. Place in a bowl and pour over the oil. Add the thyme, bay leaves and garlic and toss well. Cover with plastic wrap and marinate in the refrigerator overnight. Leave four wooden skewers to soak in water.

Heat the chargrill pan (griddle) or a barbecue. Drain the excess oil from the octopus and thread onto the skewers. Cook for 5–7 minutes on each side, or until the octopus is golden and the tip of a knife slips through a tentacle. Season with salt and pepper and drizzle with some extra marinade or extra virgin olive oil if you like. Leave for a few minutes and then serve with lemon wedges.

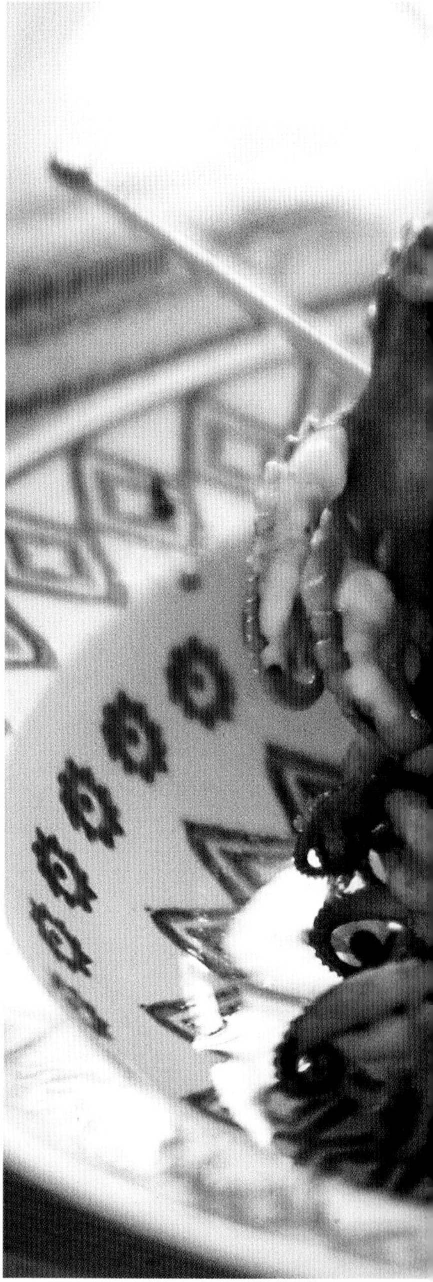

chargrilled octopus

sardine ripiene

8 medium-sized sardines, heads removed, scaled and gutted
4 tablespoons olive oil
1 small onion, thinly sliced
1 fennel bulb, thinly sliced
50 g (1/3 cup) pine nuts
4 tablespoons parsley, roughly chopped
20 g (1/4 cup) fresh breadcrumbs
1 large garlic clove, crushed
juice of 1/2 lemon
extra virgin olive oil
lemon wedges

Serves 4

Butterfly the sardines by pressing your fingers on either side of the backbone and gently easing it away from the flesh, following the line of the bone as you go. Remove the bone, leaving the tail attached to the flesh for a more attractive look. The fresher the fish, the harder this is to do, so you might want to ask your fishmonger to butterfly the sardines for you. (Alternatively, use fillets and put them back together to form a whole after cooking, although the result will not be as neat.) Rinse the fish in cold water and drain on paper towels. Leave in the fridge until needed.

Preheat the oven to 200°C (400°F/Gas 6). To prepare the stuffing, heat the olive oil in a frying pan and add the onion, fennel and pine nuts. Cook over moderately high heat until soft and light brown, stirring frequently. Mix 1 tablespoon of parsley with 1 tablespoon of breadcrumbs and set aside. Add the garlic and remaining breadcrumbs to the pan and cook for a few minutes more. Add the rest of the parsley, season and set aside. (This mixture can be made in advance and kept in the fridge, but bring back to room temperature before cooking.)

Drizzle a little olive oil in an ovenproof dish that will fit eight sardines in a single layer. Arrange the fish in the dish, skin side down, and season with salt and pepper. Spread the stuffing over the sardines and fold over to encase. (If you are using fillets, spread half with stuffing, then place the other fillets on top, skin side up, tail to tail like a sandwich.) Season again and sprinkle with the parsley and breadcrumb mixture. Drizzle with the lemon juice and a little extra virgin olive oil.

Bake for 5–10 minutes, depending on the size of the sardines. (If the filling is still warm the sardines will cook faster.) Serve immediately or at room temperature with lemon wedges.

125 ml (½ cup) extra virgin olive oil
2 garlic cloves
1 tablespoon finely chopped basil
80 ml (⅓ cup) lemon juice
12 Dublin Bay prawns (scampi or gamberoni)
12 scallops in the half shell
16 prawns (shrimp)
long sturdy twig of rosemary, for basting
16 large clams (sea dates, warty venus shells, pipis or vongole)

Serves 4

Combine the oil, garlic cloves, basil and lemon juice in a bowl and season well. Set aside to infuse for 15–20 minutes.

Remove the claws and heads from the Dublin Bay prawns, then butterfly by splitting them down the underside with a sharp knife and opening them out.

Remove the scallops from their shells, reserving the shells, and pull away the white muscle and digestive tract around each one, leaving the roes intact if you like. Peel and devein the prawns, leaving the tails intact.

Preheat a chargrill pan (griddle) or barbecue until hot. Using the rosemary twig as a brush, lightly brush the cut surfaces of the Dublin Bay prawns with the oil dressing. Brush the chargrill pan (griddle) or barbecue plate with the dressing (be careful of the flame flaring) and put the Dublin Bay prawns on to cook, shell sides down.

After 30 seconds, brush the scallops with the dressing and add them to the chargrill pan (griddle) with the prawns and clams (discard any clams that are broken or don't close when tapped). Turn the Dublin Bay prawns over and cook for another minute. Turn the prawns once. Baste with more dressing once or twice. All the shellfish should be ready within 3–4 minutes—the clams can be moved to the side and brushed with a little dressing as they open. Put the scallops back on their shells.

Discard the garlic cloves and pour the oil dressing into a small serving bowl. Transfer the shellfish to a warm serving platter. Serve at once with the dressing, bread and finger bowls.

chargrilled shellfish

olio e aceto

In every Italian restaurant, whether family-run or Milan-chic, you see the same two bottles on each table: one filled with *olio d'oliva*, olive oil, the other with *aceto*, vinegar. Used uncooked to dress a simple *insalata verde* or *mista*, these are also the liquids that flavour Italian cooking.

The fruit of Italy's ancient olive trees are gathered in the late autumn before they fully ripen, and are crushed to produce oil. The finest oils come from the first pressing and have regional flavours and complexities as wines do. In Tuscany they are a deep, fruity green, with the great estates creating unique oils from a single harvest. Pale Ligurian olive oil is more delicate, while the South, especially Puglia, produces nutty, intense oils.

Italy's finest vinegar is undoubtedly the balsamic vinegar made in Modena. Traditionally aged in wooden barrels in the city's hot attics, it improves with age and can be matured for up to a century to give a dark, concentrated liquid. The flavour is so rich it is always used sparingly and usually uncooked in a dressing, while simple red and white wine vinegars are also used for cooking and pickling.

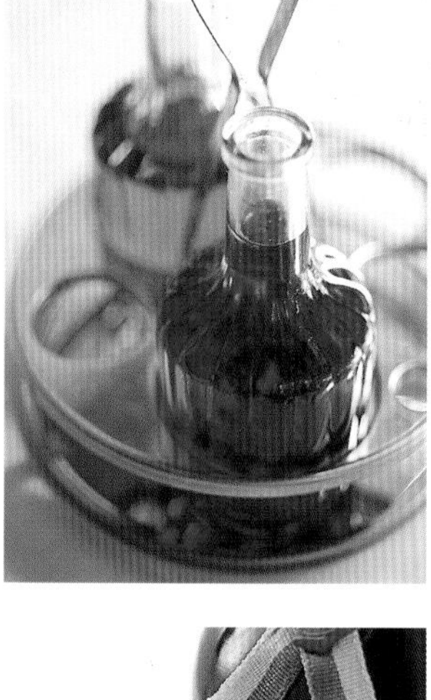

grilled quails

4 quails
2½ tablespoons lemon juice
4 tablespoons olive oil
8 small sage leaves
2 garlic cloves, halved
1 small red chilli, seeded and roughly chopped
2 tablespoons chopped parsley
lemon wedges

Serves 4

Split each quail through the breastbone with a sharp knife and then turn it over. Press open hard with the heel of your hand to form a spatchcock. Transfer the quails to a shallow dish large enough to hold all the birds side by side.

Mix together the lemon juice, olive oil, sage leaves, garlic and chilli, and season to taste with salt and pepper. Pour over the quails and leave to marinate for 30 minutes, turning the birds after 15 minutes. Preheat the grill (broiler).

Place the quails, skin side up, on a grill (broiler) tray. Position the quails 12–15 cm (4½–6 inches) below the heat and grill (broil) for about 5 minutes on each side, or until golden and cooked through. Serve hot or cold, with a sprinkling of chopped parsley and the lemon wedges.

4 large veal escalopes
plain (all-purpose) flour, seasoned with salt and pepper
1 tablespoon olive oil
2 tablespoons butter
80 ml (1/3 cup) dry white wine
250 ml (1 cup) chicken stock
3 tablespoons lemon juice
2 tablespoons capers, rinsed, and chopped if large
1 tablespoon finely chopped parsley
8 caperberries

Serves 4

Place the veal between two sheets of plastic wrap and pound with a meat mallet until an even thickness. Lightly dust each side with flour.

Heat the olive oil and butter in a large frying pan. Fry the escalopes over moderately high heat for about 2 minutes on each side, or until golden. Season and transfer to a warm plate.

Add the wine to the pan, increase the heat to high and boil until there are just 3–4 tablespoons of liquid left. Pour in the stock and boil for 4–5 minutes, or until it has reduced and slightly thickened. Add the lemon juice and capers and cook, stirring, for 1 minute. Taste for seasoning, then return the escalopes to the pan and heat through for 30 seconds. Sprinkle with parsley and serve at once, garnished with caperberries.

piccata al limone

florentine roast pork

3 large fennel bulbs
½ tablespoon finely chopped rosemary
4 garlic cloves, crushed
1 x 1.5 kg (3 lb 5 oz) pork loin, chined (bone loosened) and skinned
3 white onions
80 ml (⅓ cup) olive oil
185 ml (¾ cup) dry white wine
80 ml (⅓ cup) extra virgin olive oil
250 ml (1 cup) chicken stock
3–4 tablespoons thick (double) cream

Serves 6

Preheat the oven to 200°C (400°F/Gas 6). Cut the green fronds from the tops of the fennel and chop to give 2 tablespoons. Mix with the rosemary, garlic and plenty of salt and black pepper. Make deep incisions with a sharp knife all over the pork and rub this mixture into the incisions and the splits in the pork bone. Cut two of the onions in half and place in a roasting tin. Put the pork on top of the onion and drizzle the olive oil over the top.

Roast in the oven for 30 minutes. Baste the pork with the pan juices, then reduce the temperature to 180°C (350°F/Gas 4). Roast for another 30 minutes. Baste and lightly salt the surface of the pork. Pour in half the white wine. Roast for another 30–45 minutes, basting once or twice.

Meanwhile, remove the tough outer leaves of the fennel and discard. Slice the bulbs vertically into 1 cm (½ inch) sections and place in a large saucepan. Thinly slice the remaining onion and add to the saucepan with the extra virgin olive oil and a little salt. Add enough water to cover, put the lid on and bring to the boil. Simmer for about 45 minutes, or until the fennel is creamy and soft and almost all the liquid has evaporated.

Remove the pork from the tin and leave to rest in a warm spot. Spoon off the excess oil from the tin and discard the onion. Place the tin over high heat on the stovetop and stir in the remaining wine to deglaze. Add the stock and boil the sauce until slightly thickened. Remove from the heat, season with salt and pepper and stir in the cream. Slice the pork and serve on the fennel, with the sauce.

8 small veal escalopes
8 slices prosciutto
8 sage leaves
2 tablespoons olive oil
60 g (2¼ oz) butter
185 ml (¾ cup) dry white wine or dry Marsala

Serves 4

Place the veal between two sheets of plastic wrap and pound with a meat mallet until an even thickness. Season lightly. Cut the prosciutto slices to the same size as the veal. Cover each piece of veal with a slice of prosciutto and place a sage leaf on top. Secure in place with a cocktail stick.

Heat the oil and half the butter in a large frying pan. Add the veal in batches and fry, prosciutto up, over moderately high heat for 3–4 minutes, or until the veal is just cooked through. Transfer each batch to a hot plate as it is done.

Pour off the oil from the pan and add the wine. Cook over high heat until reduced by half, scraping up the bits from the bottom of the pan. Add the remaining butter and, when it has melted, season. Spoon over the veal to serve.

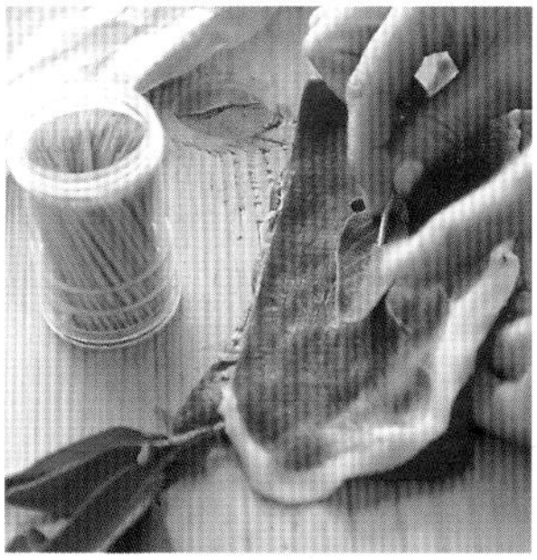

veal saltimbocca

osso bucco alla milanese

12 pieces veal shank, about 4 cm (1½ inches) thick
plain (all-purpose) flour, seasoned with salt and pepper
60 ml (¼ cup) olive oil
60 g (2¼ oz) butter
1 garlic clove
250 ml (1 cup) dry white wine
1 bay leaf or lemon leaf
pinch of allspice
pinch of ground cinnamon

GREMOLATA
2 teaspoons grated lemon zest
6 tablespoons finely chopped parsley
1 garlic clove, finely chopped

thin lemon wedges

Serves 4

Tie each piece of veal shank around its girth to secure the flesh, then dust with the seasoned flour. Heat the oil, butter and garlic in a large heavy saucepan big enough to hold the shanks in a single layer. Put the shanks in the pan and cook for 12–15 minutes until well browned. Arrange the shanks, standing them up in a single layer, pour in the wine and add the bay leaf, allspice and cinnamon. Cover the saucepan.

Cook at a low simmer for 15 minutes, then add 125 ml (½ cup) warm water. Continue cooking, covered, for about 45 minutes to 1 hour (the timing will depend on the age of the veal) until the meat is tender and you can cut it with a fork. Check the volume of liquid once or twice and add more warm water as needed. Transfer the veal to a plate and keep warm. Discard the garlic clove and bay leaf.

To make the gremolata, mix together the lemon zest, parsley and garlic. Increase the heat under the saucepan and stir for 1–2 minutes until the sauce is thick, scraping up any bits off the bottom of the saucepan as you stir. Stir in the gremolata. Season with salt and pepper if necessary, then return the veal to the sauce. Heat through, then serve with the lemon wedges.

8 asparagus spears
4 veal escalopes
4 thin slices mortadella (preferably with pistachio nuts)
4 thin slices Bel Paese cheese
plain (all-purpose) flour, seasoned with salt and pepper
3 tablespoons butter
1 tablespoon olive oil
3 tablespoons dry Marsala

Serves 4

Wash the asparagus and remove the woody ends (hold each spear at both ends and bend it gently—it will snap at its natural breaking point). Blanch the asparagus in boiling salted water for 3 minutes. Drain, reserving 3 tablespoons of the liquid.

Place each veal escalope between two sheets of plastic wrap and pound with a meat mallet to make a 12 x 18 cm (5 x 7 inch) rectangle. Season lightly with salt and pepper. Trim both the mortadella and cheese slices to just a little smaller than the veal.

Cover each piece of veal with a slice of mortadella, then a slice of cheese. Place an asparagus spear in the centre, running across the shortest width, with the tip slightly overhanging the veal at one end. Place another asparagus spear alongside, but with its tip overhanging the other end. Roll each veal slice up tightly and tie in place at each end with kitchen string. Roll in the seasoned flour to coat.

Heat 2 tablespoons of the butter with the olive oil in a frying pan. Fry the rolls over low heat for about 10 minutes, turning frequently, until golden and tender. Transfer to a hot serving dish and keep warm.

Add the Marsala, the reserved asparagus liquid and the remaining butter to the pan and bring quickly to the boil. Simmer for 3–4 minutes, scraping up the bits from the base of the pan. The juices will reduce and darken. Taste for seasoning, then spoon over the veal rolls and serve immediately.

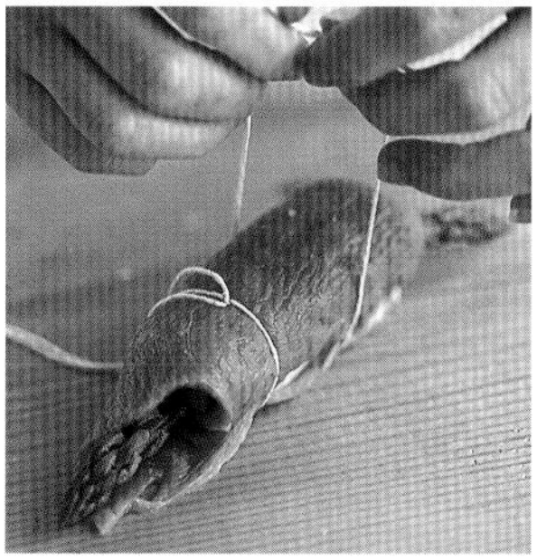

veal involtini

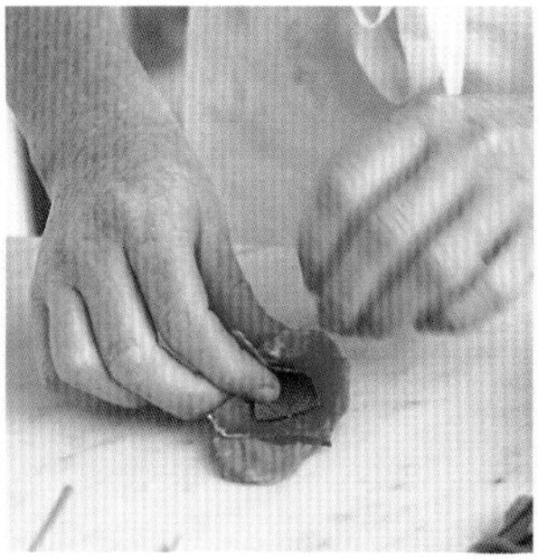

uccelletti scappati

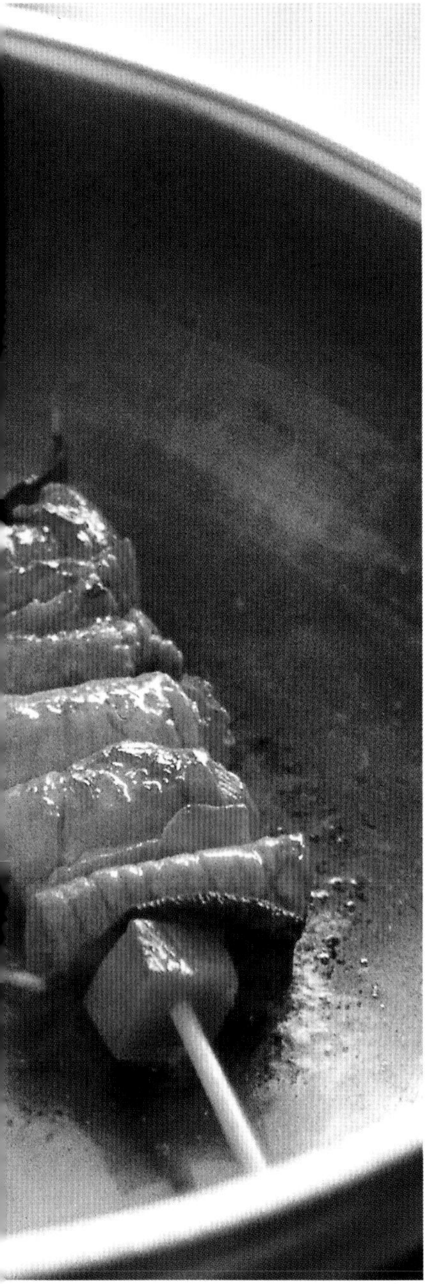

650 g (1 lb 7 oz) sliced leg of veal
90 g (3¼ oz) pancetta, thinly sliced
50–60 sage leaves
90 g (3¼ oz) pancetta, cubed
75 g (2½ oz) butter

Serves 6

Soak 12 bamboo skewers in cold water for 1 hour.

Place the veal between two sheets of plastic wrap and pound with a meat mallet until an even thickness. Cut into 6 x 3 cm (2½ x 1¼ inch) rectangles and trim the pancetta slices to the same size.

Working in batches, place the veal pieces out flat on a board and season with pepper. Place a slice of pancetta on each rectangle of veal and then half a sage leaf on top. Roll each veal slice up, starting from one of the shortest ends.

Thread a cube of pancetta onto a skewer, followed by a sage leaf. Thread the skewer through a veal roll to prevent it unrolling. Thread four more veal rolls onto the skewer, followed by a sage leaf and, finally, another cube of pancetta. Continue in this way with more skewers until all the ingredients are used.

Heat the butter in a large frying pan. When it foams, add the skewers in batches and cook over high heat for about 12 minutes, or until cooked through, turning several times during cooking. Season lightly and serve with fried polenta.

vino... As regional as Italian food, and seen as its partner in every way, wine is hardly ever drunk alone in Italy. Instead, a meal is accompanied by a *mezzo* (half-litre) of local *rosso* or *bianco*, the same one used in the kitchen for braising a cut of beef or adding to a pot of *osso bucco.* Every part of Italy is a wine region, and every area produces its own *vini da tavola*, usually quite drinkable and rarely bottled. These wines are highly individual, small independent producers predominate and the terrain, grape varieties and microclimates can produce wines that are endlessly variable. These are the

wines to partner the local food, totally without pretension, they are taken from the same terrain that nurtures the vegetables sold in the market and the wheat that is turned daily into bread and pasta.

Bottles of wine are mostly limited to the best an area has to offer and they are found more often in Italy's great wine-producing regions. Barolo and Barbaresco from Piemonte and Chianti Classico and Brunello di Montalcino from Tuscany are among Italy's finest reds, while Friuli and Alto Adige on the northern borders produce whites of real character.

Drinking outside Italy, the situation can be very different. Poor bottles of wine are mass-produced for export, tainting many fine names from Lambrusco and Soave to Valpolicella. Forced to implement stricter controls, Italy introduced a DOCG classification in the 1980s, similar to France's *Appellation Contrôlée,* and its wines are now among Italy's best. At the same time, the rigidities and constraints of the new classification led to a number of prestigious wines falling outside the system. Remaining as simple *vini da tavola,* these highly crafted, individual wines go by the nickname 'the Supertuscans' and are among Italy's most prized and sought-after wines.

750 g (1 lb 10 oz) trimmed thick beef fillet
3 garlic cloves, thinly sliced
2 tablespoons chopped rosemary
8–10 thin slices prosciutto, pancetta or smoked bacon
2 tablespoons olive oil
20 g (1 oz) dried wild mushrooms, such as porcini
1 onion, halved and sliced
170 ml (2/3 cup) red wine such as Barolo
400 g (14 oz) tin chopped tomatoes

Serves 4

Make several small incisions around the beef. Push a slice of garlic into each incision, using up one of the garlic cloves. Scatter 1 tablespoon of rosemary over the beef and season with salt and pepper. Lay the prosciutto slices on a board in a line next to each other, creating a sheet of prosciutto to wrap the beef in. Put the beef fillet across them and fold the prosciutto over to enclose the fillet. Tie several times with kitchen string to keep the beef and prosciutto together. Leave in the fridge to rest for at least 15 minutes.

Preheat the oven to 190°C (375°F/Gas 5). Heat the olive oil in a casserole. Add the beef and sear on all sides until the prosciutto is golden brown, but not burnt. A little of the prosciutto might fall off, but it doesn't matter: just make sure the beef is well sealed. Remove from the casserole.

Soak the mushrooms in 185 ml (3/4 cup) hot water for 10 minutes. Add the onion to the casserole, reduce the heat and gently cook until soft. Add the remaining garlic and rosemary and cook for a few minutes more.

Remove the mushrooms from the water and add to the onion, reserving the water. Cook the mushrooms for a couple of minutes, then add the mushroom water, discarding any sediment at the bottom of the bowl, and boil until nearly all the liquid is reduced. Add the wine and cook for a few minutes, then add the tomato and cook for another 5–10 minutes to reduce to a thick sauce.

Season with salt and pepper and add the beef to the casserole, turning over in the sauce to coat all sides. Cover the casserole with a lid and place in the oven. Cook the beef for 15 minutes for rare or 20 minutes for medium-rare. Remove from the oven and leave to rest, covered, for at least 15 minutes.

beef braised in red wine

fagioli all'uccelletto

350 g (12 oz) dried cannellini beans
bouquet garni
125 ml (½ cup) olive oil
2 garlic cloves
1 sprig of sage, or ½ teaspoon dried sage
4 ripe tomatoes, peeled and chopped
1 tablespoon balsamic vinegar

Serves 6

Soak the beans in cold water overnight, then drain. Place in a large saucepan of cold water with the bouquet garni and bring to the boil. Add 2 tablespoons of the olive oil, reduce the heat and simmer for 1 hour. Add 1 teaspoon of salt and 500 ml (2 cups) boiling water and cook for another 30 minutes, or until tender. Drain.

Cut the garlic cloves in half and put them in a large saucepan with the sage and the remaining oil. Gently heat to infuse the flavours, but do not fry. Add the tomato and simmer for 10 minutes, then discard the garlic and the sprig of sage.

Add the beans, season well and simmer for 15 minutes. Add a little boiling water at first to keep the pan moist, but then let the liquid evaporate towards the end of cooking. Stir the vinegar through just before serving. Serve hot.

2 heads radicchio
60 ml (1/4 cup) olive oil
1 teaspoon balsamic vinegar

Serves 4

Trim the radicchio, discarding the outer leaves. Slice into quarters lengthways and rinse well. Drain, then pat dry with paper towels.

Preheat a chargrill pan (griddle) to hot. Lightly sprinkle the radicchio with some of the olive oil and season. Cook for 2–3 minutes, until the under leaves soften and darken, then turn to cook the other side. Transfer to a dish and sprinkle with the remaining oil and vinegar. Serve hot with grilled (broiled) meats, or cold as part of an antipasto platter.

grilled radicchio

potato cake

1 small onion, thinly sliced into rings
75 g (2½ oz) butter
2 garlic cloves, crushed
1 kg (2 lb 4 oz) potatoes, thinly sliced
100 g (3½ oz) mozzarella cheese, grated
50 g (½ cup) grated Parmesan cheese
2 tablespoons milk

Serves 4

Put the onion in a bowl, cover with cold water and leave for 1 hour. Drain well. Preheat the oven to 210°C (415°F/Gas 6–7). Line a 20 cm (8 inch) springform cake tin with foil. Grease the foil.

Melt the butter in a small saucepan, add the garlic and set aside. Place a layer of potato over the base of the tin, followed by layers of onion, butter, mozzarella and Parmesan. Repeat the layers until you have used up all the ingredients, finishing with potato and keeping a bit of butter to drizzle on at the end. Season the layers as you go. Spoon the milk over the top.

Bake for 1 hour, or until the top is golden brown and the potatoes are tender. If the top is overbrowning before the potatoes are done, cover with foil. Cool for 10 minutes before serving. Unclip the base of the tin, peel off the foil and transfer to a warm plate for serving.

a little taste of...

Cucina casalinga is Italy's home-style cooking, the food cooked every day by women in their kitchens, making use of vegetables and herbs picked from the garden or bought fresh in the morning—beans and lentils, and pieces of the family's own cured meat, chicken or a wild rabbit. It is also the food served in Italy's many family-run trattorie and *osterie*, restaurants that replicate the good cooking of the home. Many of the recipes have their roots in peasant food, *cucina povera,* but *cucina casalinga* also includes dishes such as young tender lamb or pork cooked with herbs over the fire, or autumn game braised with olives, the ingredients more varied, but still simple food prepared with care. Each region has its own *cucina casalinga*, but throughout the country recipes tend to include inexpensive vegetables such as potatoes, tomatoes and cabbages, along with beans and day-old bread. The Tuscan soup *la ribollita* is quintessential *cucina casalinga*—vegetables, beans and herbs thickened with bread and drizzled with the area's fruity olive oil.

...cucina casalinga

marinated fresh anchovies

400 g (14 oz) fresh anchovies
60 ml (¼ cup) olive oil
1 tablespoon extra virgin olive oil
3 tablespoons lemon juice
2 garlic cloves, crushed
2 tablespoons finely chopped parsley
2 tablespoons finely chopped basil
1 small red chilli, seeded and chopped

Serves 4

Fillet the anchovies by running your thumbnail or a sharp knife along the backbone, then pulling the head upwards. The head, bones and guts should all come away together, leaving you with the fillets. Carefully wash under cold water and pat dry with paper towels. Place the fillets in a shallow serving dish.

Mix all the remaining ingredients together with some salt and pepper and pour over the anchovies. Cover with plastic wrap and marinate in the fridge for at least 3 hours before serving.

250 g (9 oz) dried chickpeas
3 tablespoons olive oil
1 large onion, finely chopped
1 celery stalk, finely chopped
1 carrot, finely chopped
2 garlic cloves, crushed
1 sprig of rosemary
pinch of crushed dried chilli
2 tablespoons tomato paste (purée)
1.5 litres (6 cups) vegetable stock
125 g (4½ oz) small pasta shells
drizzle of extra virgin olive oil
grated Parmesan cheese

Serves 4

Put the chickpeas in a large saucepan, cover with cold water and soak overnight. Drain and rinse under cold water.

Heat the olive oil in a large saucepan, add the chopped vegetables, garlic and rosemary and cook over moderately low heat for 8 minutes. Add the chilli and season. Stir in the tomato paste and stock, then add the chickpeas. Bring to the boil. Reduce the heat and simmer for 1–1½ hours, or until the chickpeas are tender, adding a little boiling water every so often to maintain the level.

Add the pasta and continue cooking until it is *al dente*. Remove the sprig of rosemary. Drizzle with extra virgin olive oil and sprinkle with Parmesan.

pasta e ceci

tagliatelle with ragù

60 g (2¼ oz) butter
1 onion, finely chopped
1 celery stalk, finely chopped
1 carrot, finely chopped
90 g (3¼ oz) pancetta or bacon, finely chopped
220 g (8 oz) minced (ground) beef
220 g (8 oz) minced (ground) pork
2 sprigs of oregano, chopped, or ¼ teaspoon dried oregano
pinch of nutmeg
120 g (4½ oz) chicken livers, trimmed and finely chopped
125 ml (½ cup) dry white wine
185 ml (¾ cup) milk
400 g (14 oz) tin chopped tomatoes
250 ml (1 cup) beef stock
400 g (14 oz) tagliatelle
grated Parmesan cheese

Serves 4

Melt the butter in a saucepan and add the onion, celery, carrot and pancetta. Cook over moderate heat for 6–8 minutes, stirring from time to time.

Add the minced beef, pork and oregano to the saucepan. Season with salt and pepper and the nutmeg. Cook for about 5 minutes, or until the mince has changed colour but not browned. Add the chicken liver and cook until it changes colour.

Pour in the wine, increase the heat and boil over high heat for 2–3 minutes, or until the wine has been absorbed. Stir in 125 ml (½ cup) of the milk, reduce the heat and simmer for 10 minutes. Add the tomato and half the stock, partially cover the pan and leave to simmer gently over very low heat for 3 hours. Add more of the stock as it is needed to keep the sauce moist.

Meanwhile, cook the tagliatelle in a large saucepan of boiling salted water until *al dente*. Stir the remaining milk into the sauce 5 minutes before serving. Taste the sauce for seasoning, then drain the tagliatelle, toss with the sauce and serve with grated Parmesan.

1 garlic clove, cut in half
1 loaf 'country-style' bread, such as ciabatta
6 ripe tomatoes
1 small yellow capsicum (pepper)
½ cucumber, peeled
½ white salad onion
2 tablespoons shredded basil leaves
80 ml (⅓ cup) olive oil
2 tablespoons red wine vinegar

Serves 4

Rub the cut side of the garlic around the inside of a large salad bowl. Remove the crust from the bread and cut it into cubes. Put the bread in the bowl and sprinkle it with enough cold water to moisten.

Cut the tomatoes, capsicum and cucumber into chunks and dice the onion. Add the vegetables to the bread with the basil and then sprinkle with the olive oil and vinegar. Toss well and leave for 30 minutes before serving.

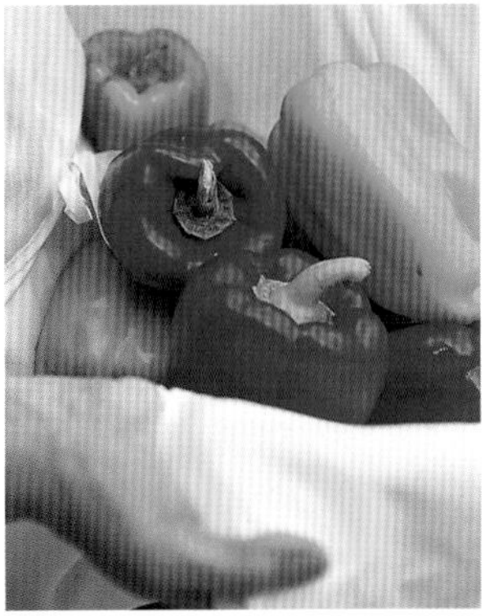

panzanella

street markets

In Italy, markets and food shops go hand-in-hand, with stalls shadowing the narrow streets, squeezed in between the *panificio* (bakery) or *pescheria* (fishmonger). Cities may also have a *Piazza Erbe*, an open square ringed by *gelaterie* and bars, where the *mercato* provides the city's wake-up call. Wonderfully regional, the markets vary even from one town to the next. Salty capers, just-picked oranges and fat, purple eggplants (aubergines) are to be found in the labyrinth of Sicily's Mediterranean Vucciria market, while artichokes dominate the stalls in the

beautiful Campo de'Fiori in Rome. In Venice, the produce is more northern European, with radicchio, savoy cabbage and white asparagus brought in by boat to the Rialto market. A tribute to Italy's rural traditions, and the small-scale producers who understand their land and what grows best, the produce is often organic, though never labelled as such, and always seasonal. In the spring, there are early crops of tender young vegetables, from peas to asparagus, while in the autumn, local funghi, piled high on stalls and in trucks, is eagerly awaited.

lasagne al forno

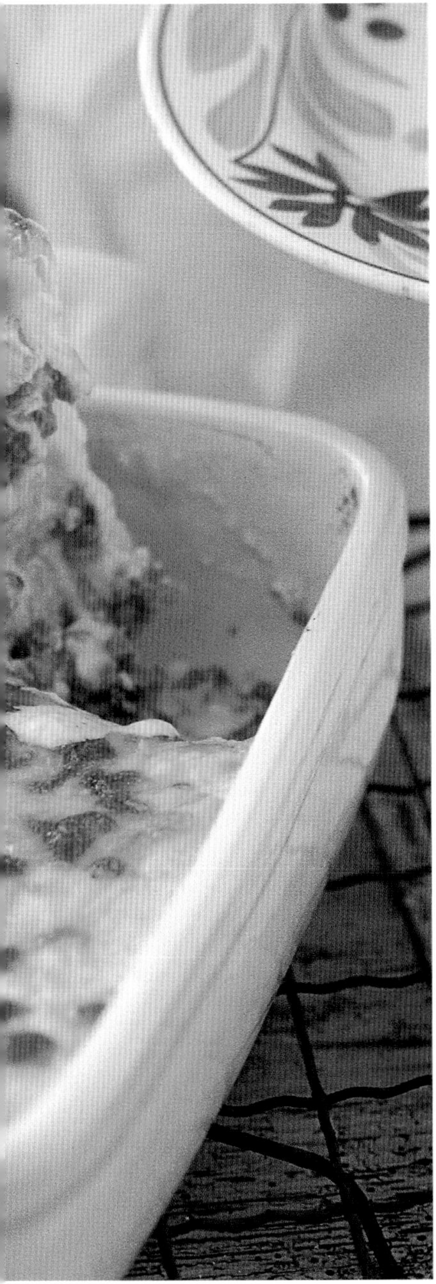

MEAT SAUCE
30 g (1 oz) butter
1 onion, finely chopped
1 small carrot, finely chopped
½ celery stalk, finely chopped
1 garlic clove, crushed
120 g (4½ oz) pancetta, sliced
500 g (1 lb 2 oz) minced (ground) beef
¼ teaspoon dried oregano
pinch of ground nutmeg
90 g (3¼ oz) chicken livers, trimmed and finely chopped
4 tablespoons dry vermouth or white wine
350 ml (1⅓ cups) beef stock
1 tablespoon tomato paste (purée)
2 tablespoons thick (double) cream
1 egg, beaten

1 quantity béchamel sauce (page 251)
125 ml (½ cup) thick (double) cream
100 g (3½ oz) fresh lasagne verde or 6 sheets dried lasagne
150 g (1 cup) grated mozzarella cheese
60 g (⅔ cup) grated Parmesan cheese

Serves 6

To make the meat sauce, heat the butter in a frying pan and add the chopped vegetables, garlic and pancetta. Cook over moderately low heat for 5–6 minutes, or until softened and light golden. Add the beef, increase the heat a little and cook for 8 minutes, or until coloured but not browned, stirring to break up the lumps. Add the oregano and nutmeg and season well.

Stir in the chicken liver and cook until it changes colour. Pour in the vermouth, increase the heat and cook until it has evaporated. Add the beef stock and tomato paste and simmer for 2 hours. Add a little hot water, if necessary, during this time to keep the mixture moist, but towards the end let all the liquid be absorbed. Stir in the cream, remove from the heat and leave to cool for 15 minutes. Stir in the egg.

Put the béchamel in a saucepan, heat gently and stir in the cream. Remove from the heat and cool slightly. Preheat the oven to 180°C (350°F/Gas 4) and grease a 22 x 15 x 7 cm (9 x 6 x 2¾ inch) ovenproof dish.

If using fresh pasta, cut into manageable sheets and cook in a large saucepan of boiling salted water until *al dente*. Scoop out each batch with a slotted spoon as it is done, drop into a bowl of cold water, then spread out on a tea towel to dry. Spread half the meat sauce in the dish. Scatter with half the mozzarella, then cover with a slightly overlapping layer of pasta sheets. Spread half the béchamel over this and sprinkle with half the Parmesan. Repeat the layers, finishing with a layer of béchamel and Parmesan. Bake for about 40 minutes until golden brown and leave to rest for 10 minutes before serving.

220 g (8 oz) dried borlotti beans
50 g (1¾ oz) lard or butter
1 large onion, finely chopped
1 garlic clove, finely chopped
15 g (½ oz) parsley, finely chopped
2 sage leaves
100 g (3½ oz) pancetta, cubed
2 celery stalks, halved then sliced
2 carrots, sliced
3 potatoes, peeled but left whole
1 teaspoon tomato paste (purée)
400 g (14 oz) tin chopped tomatoes
8 basil leaves
3 litres (12 cups) chicken or vegetable stock
2 zucchini (courgettes), sliced
220 g (8 oz) shelled peas
120 g (4 oz) runner beans, cut into short lengths
¼ cabbage, shredded
150 g (5½ oz) ditalini, avemarie or other small pasta
1 quantity pesto (page 251)
grated Parmesan cheese

Serves 6

Put the dried beans in a large bowl, cover with cold water and leave to soak overnight. Drain and rinse under cold water.

To make the soffritto, melt the lard in a large saucepan and add the onion, garlic, parsley, sage and pancetta. Cook over low heat, stirring once or twice, for about 10 minutes, or until the onion is soft and golden.

Add the celery, carrot and potatoes and cook for 5 minutes. Stir in the tomato paste, tomato, basil and borlotti beans. Season with plenty of pepper. Add the stock and bring slowly to the boil. Cover and leave to simmer for 2 hours, stirring once or twice.

If the potatoes haven't already broken up, roughly break them up with a fork against the side of the pan. Taste for seasoning and add the zucchini, peas, runner beans, cabbage and pasta. Simmer until the pasta is *al dente*. Serve with a dollop of pesto and the Parmesan.

minestrone alla genovese

la ribollita

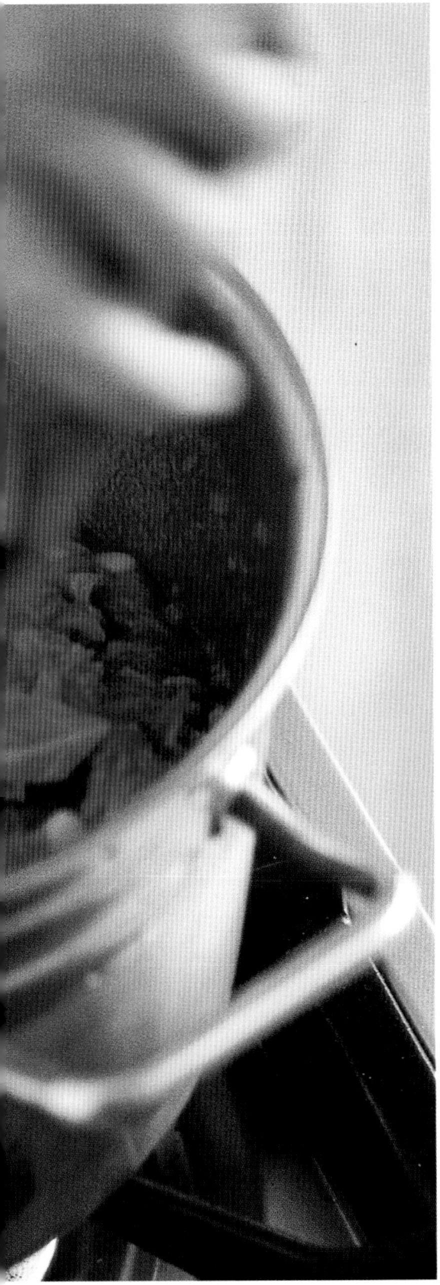

4 tablespoons olive oil
1 onion, finely chopped
1 large carrot, finely chopped
3 celery stalks, finely chopped
2 large garlic cloves, crushed
250 g (9 oz) cavolo nero or savoy cabbage
1 zucchini (courgette), finely chopped
400 g (14 oz) cooked cannellini or borlotti beans
400 g (14 oz) tin tomatoes
185 ml (3/4 cup) red wine
1 litre (4 cups) chicken stock or water
75 g (2 1/2 oz) stale 'country-style' bread, such as ciabatta or pugliese, crusts removed and broken into 2.5 cm (1 inch) cubes
drizzle of extra virgin olive oil

Serves 4

To make the soffritto, pour the olive oil into a large saucepan and add the onion. Cook the onion gently—use this time to chop the carrot and celery and add them to the pan as you go along. Once you have added the garlic, leave to cook for a few minutes.

Strip the leaves of the cavolo from the stems or cut away the thick stem of the savoy. Wash and finely chop the stems and roughly chop the leaves. Add the cabbage stems and zucchini to the soffritto and cook, stirring occasionally, for about 5 minutes, or until the vegetables have changed to an opaque colour and soaked up some of the olive oil.

Stir in the beans and cook for 5 minutes more, then add the tomato and cook for another 5 minutes to reduce the liquid.

Add the cabbage leaves and mix into the soup, stirring until just wilted. Add the wine and stock or water and gently simmer for about 40 minutes.

Add the bread to the pan (if the bread is very fresh, dry it out a little in the oven first to prevent it disintegrating into the soup). Mix briefly and remove the pan from the heat. Leave for about 30 minutes. This rests the soup and allows the flavours to mingle. Serve hot, but not boiling, with a generous drizzle of extra virgin olive oil.

If reheating the soup, make sure it comes to the boil but then remove it from the heat and leave to cool for 5 minutes. Serve in cold bowls. The soup should be warm, rather than piping hot.

2 tablespoons olive oil
3 garlic cloves, crushed
1 white onion, finely chopped
900 g (2 lb) ripe tomatoes, peeled and finely chopped
200 g (7 oz) stale 'country-style' bread, such as ciabatta, thickly sliced and crusts removed
850 ml (3 1/3 cups) hot chicken stock
20 basil leaves, shredded
drizzle of extra virgin olive oil

Serves 4

Heat the olive oil in a large saucepan. Add the garlic and onion and cook over low heat for 6–8 minutes, or until softened but not browned. Add the tomato and season. Cover and simmer for 30 minutes. Break the bread into pieces and add to the saucepan. Simmer, stirring once or twice, for 5 minutes.

Gradually stir in the stock. Cook, stirring, until the bread has broken down and the soup is thick. Remove from the heat and add the basil. Cover and leave for 1 hour. Serve at room temperature or reheat. Drizzle extra virgin olive oil into each bowl before serving.

pappa al pomodoro

mushroom and fennel omelette

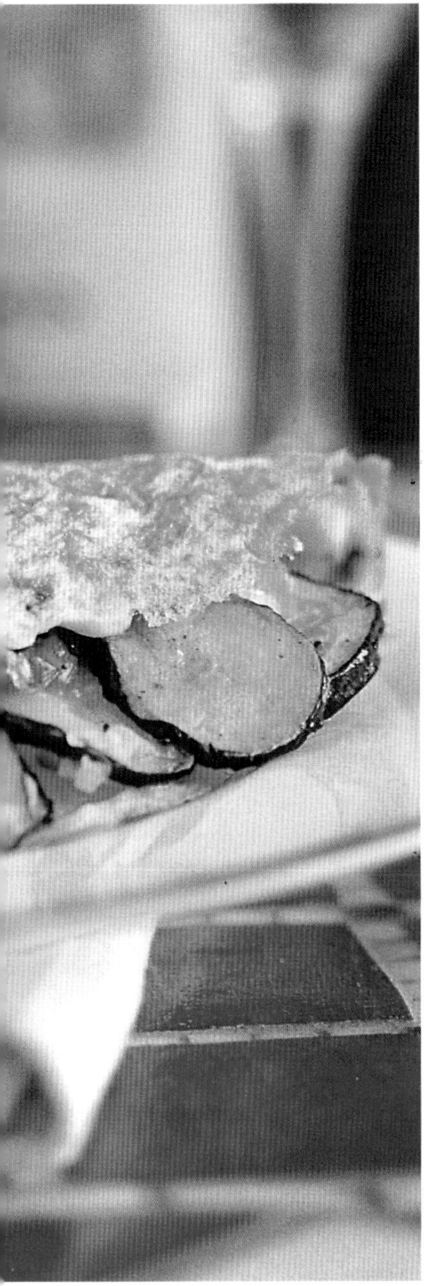

3 tablespoons butter
100 g (3½ oz) button mushrooms, sliced
1 baby fennel bulb, thinly sliced (reserving the fronds)
1½ tablespoons olive oil
6 eggs

Serves 2

Melt 2 tablespoons of the butter in a small frying pan and cook the mushrooms and fennel for 4–5 minutes, until the fennel has softened and the mushrooms are lightly golden. Season and remove from the pan.

Heat the remaining butter with the oil in a small frying pan. Beat the eggs and stir in 1½ tablespoons of chopped fennel fronds. Season well. Pour the eggs into the frying pan and cook gently over high heat, pulling the mixture in from the sides until it begins to set in small, fluffy clumps. Reduce the heat and shake the pan from side to side to prevent the omelette sticking.

When the omelette is almost set but still soft on the surface, spoon the mushroom mixture onto one half, then fold the omelette over to cover the mushrooms. Cook for 10–12 seconds, shaking the pan once or twice. Slide the omelette onto a warm plate and serve at once.

PASTRY
220 g (1¾ cups) plain all-purpose flour
½ teaspoon baking powder
pinch of salt
100 g (3½ oz) butter, chilled
55 g (¼ cup) caster (superfine) sugar
1 egg yolk
60 ml (¼ cup) cream

FILLING
500 g (1 lb 2 oz) ricotta cheese
3 eggs
50 g (½ cup) grated pecorino Romano cheese
100 g (⅔ cup) grated mozzarella cheese
125 g (4½ oz) prosciutto, finely shredded
2 tablespoons finely chopped parsley

Serves 6

To make the pastry, sift the flour, baking powder and salt into a large bowl. Cut the butter into cubes and add it to the bowl, then rub it in with your fingertips until the mixture resembles fine breadcrumbs. Stir in the sugar.

Mix the egg yolk and cream together and pour this into the pastry mixture. Mix together and then knead once or twice until you have a soft dough. Refrigerate until needed.

To make the filling, mix the ricotta with the eggs, cheese, prosciutto and parsley and season well with pepper—you probably won't need to add any salt if the prosciutto is salty. Preheat the oven to 200°C (400°F/Gas 6).

Cut one-third off the pastry and roll out the remainder on a floured surface. Line a 20 x 4 cm (8 x 1½ inch) pie tin and trim off any excess pastry. Fill the pastry case with the filling and smooth the top.

Roll out the remaining pastry and cover the pie. Trim the edges and bake for 20 minutes, then reduce the temperature to 180°C (350°F/Gas 4) and bake for another 20 minutes, or until the filling is cooked through.

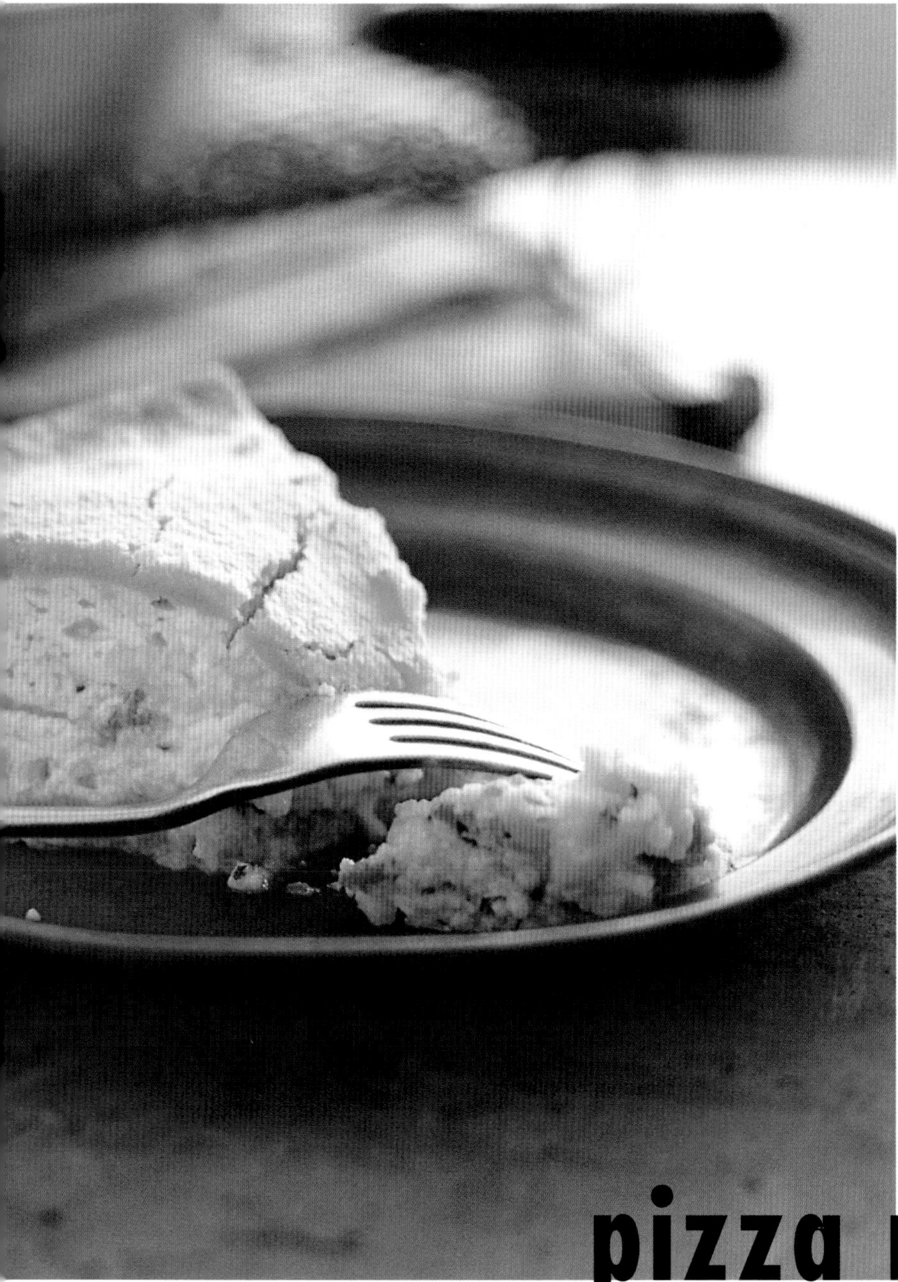

pizza rustica

baked swordfish siciliana

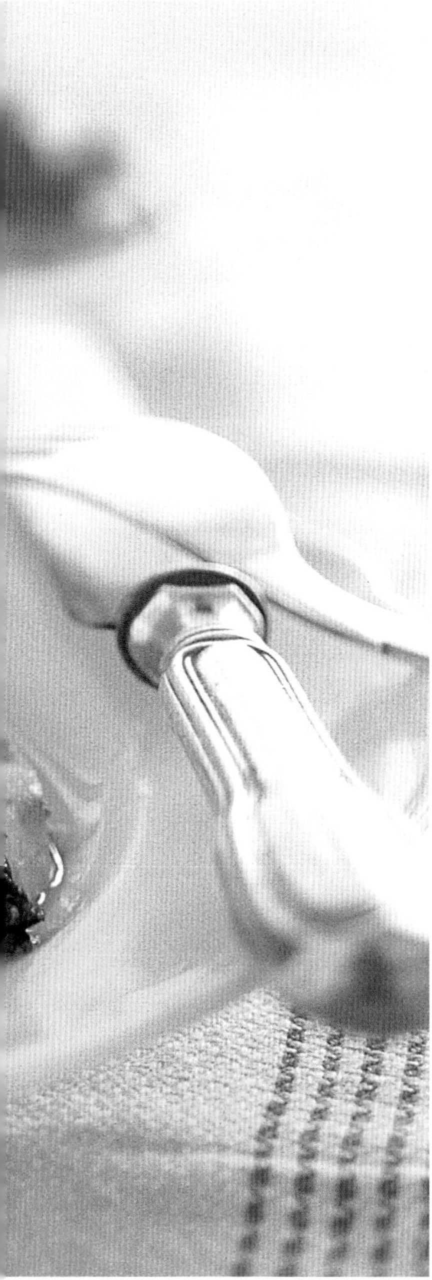

80 ml (1/3 cup) olive oil
2 tablespoons lemon juice
2 1/2 tablespoons finely chopped basil
4 swordfish steaks
60 g (2 1/4 oz) pitted black olives, chopped
1 tablespoon baby capers
1/2 teaspoon finely chopped anchovies in olive oil
400 g (14 oz) tomatoes, peeled, seeded and chopped
2 tablespoons dried breadcrumbs

Serves 4

Mix half the olive oil with the lemon juice and 1 tablespoon of the basil. Season and pour into a shallow ovenproof dish, large enough to hold the swordfish in a single layer. Arrange the swordfish in the dish and leave to marinate for 15 minutes, turning once. Preheat the oven to 230°C (450°F/Gas 8) and preheat the grill (broiler).

Combine the olives, capers, anchovies and tomato with the remaining olive oil and basil and season well. Spread over the swordfish and sprinkle the breadcrumbs over the top. Bake for about 20 minutes, or until the fish is just opaque. Finish off by placing briefly under the hot grill (broiler) until the breadcrumbs are crisp. Serve with bread to soak up the juices.

400 g (14 oz) dried beans, such as cannellini
1 bay leaf
1 garlic clove
125 ml (½ cup) olive oil
1 small red onion, finely sliced
2 tablespoons finely chopped parsley
400 g (14 oz) tin tuna in olive oil, drained

Serves 4

Soak the beans overnight in plenty of cold water. Rinse them and transfer to a very large saucepan. Cover with plenty of cold water and bring to the boil. Add the bay leaf, garlic and 1 tablespoon of the olive oil, cover and simmer for 1–1½ hours or until tender, depending on the age of the beans. Salt the water for the last 15–20 minutes of cooking. The beans should keep their shape and have a slight bite rather than being soft.

Drain well, remove the bay leaf and garlic and transfer the beans to a shallow serving dish. Add the onion and remaining olive oil and season with salt and pepper. Toss well, then chill.

Toss through two-thirds of the parsley and taste for seasoning. Break the tuna up into bite-sized pieces and toss through the beans. Sprinkle the remaining parsley over the top and serve.

tuna with beans

chicken cacciatora

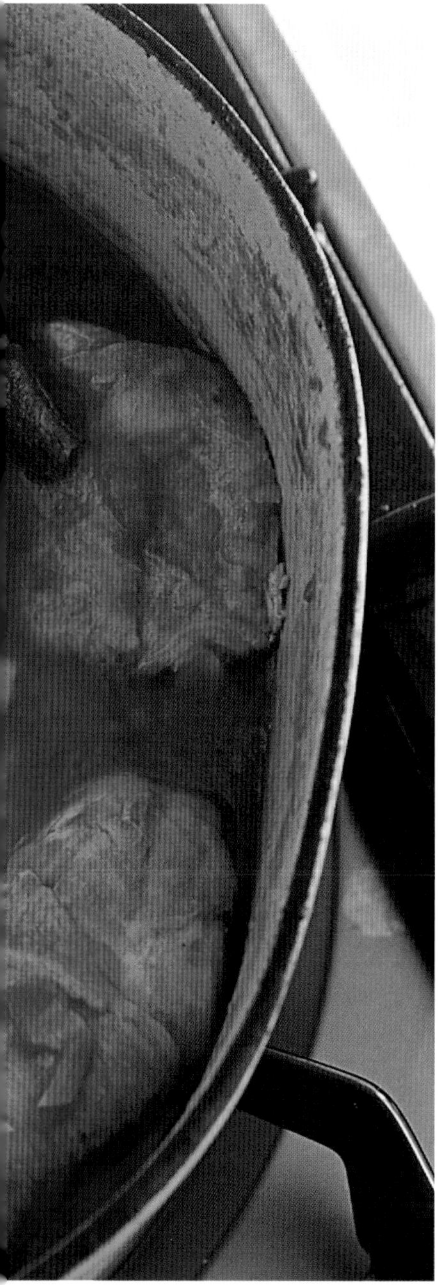

3 tablespoons olive oil
1 large onion, finely chopped
3 garlic cloves, crushed
1 celery stalk, finely chopped
150 g (5½ oz) pancetta, finely chopped
125 g (4½ oz) button mushrooms, thickly sliced
4 chicken drumsticks
4 chicken thighs
80 ml (⅓ cup) dry vermouth or dry white wine
2 x 400 g (14 oz) tins chopped tomatoes
¼ teaspoon brown sugar
1 sprig of oregano, plus 4–5 sprigs to garnish
1 sprig of rosemary
1 bay leaf

Serves 4

Heat half the oil in a large casserole. Add the onion, garlic and celery and cook, stirring from time to time, over moderately low heat for 6–8 minutes, until the onion is golden.

Add the pancetta and mushrooms, increase the heat and cook, stirring occasionally, for 4–5 minutes. Spoon out onto a plate and set aside.

Add the remaining olive oil to the casserole and lightly brown the chicken pieces, a few at a time. Season them as they brown. Spoon off any excess fat and return all the pieces to the casserole. Add the vermouth, increase the heat and cook until the liquid has almost evaporated.

Add the tomato, sugar, oregano, rosemary, bay leaf and 80 ml (⅓ cup) cold water. Bring to the boil, then stir in the reserved pancetta mixture. Cover and leave to simmer for 20 minutes, or until the chicken is tender but not falling off the bone.

If the liquid is too thin, remove the chicken from the casserole, increase the heat and boil until thickened. Discard the sprigs of herbs and taste for salt and pepper. Toss in the additional oregano sprigs and the dish is ready to serve.

cucina povera

Cucina povera, 'the food of the poor', holds an extraordinary fascination for Italians. Searching for the classic dishes of Italian gastronomy, restaurateurs, food writers and food lovers have begun to celebrate, and often romanticize, the traditional peasant dishes of the countryside, and the ingenuity used to create such an imaginative diet from an often harsh land.

At the heart of *cucina povera* is the indigenous ingredients that were available freely to rich and poor. Fantastic funghi, harvested from woodland by families in the autumn, were eaten fresh or dried and saved for the winter. Dandelion, wild greens, fennel, asparagus and rocket (arugula) were gathered up and eaten raw or cooked in a little oil or fat; and the food of the *cacciatore*, the hunter—wild boar, rabbit and fowl—were prized.

Each region has its own *cucina povera*, from the sustaining stews and soups of Tuscany and Umbria, the meat filled out with beans, lentils and *cavolo nero*, Tuscan black cabbage, to the imaginative vegetarian cooking of the South, with its wonderful tomatoes and blistered grilled capsicums (peppers) and eggplants (aubergines). The offal dishes served in the restaurants of Rome's old working-class Testaccio district, once home to the city's slaughterhouse, point to another legacy of *cucina povera*. Here workers' meagre salaries were once topped up with the *quinto quarto*, or fifth quarter, the least desirable parts of the day's slaughter. The dishes created from these humble leftovers are now among Italy's most celebrated.

2 sprigs of rosemary
3 garlic cloves
1 teaspoon balsamic vinegar
1.5 kg (3 lb 5 oz) chicken
2 tablespoons extra virgin olive oil
2 tablespoons olive oil
125 ml (½ cup) chicken stock

Serves 4

Preheat the oven to 200°C (400°F/Gas 6). Put one rosemary sprig, the garlic and balsamic vinegar inside the cavity of the chicken. Add a large pinch of salt and a few grinds of black pepper. Truss the legs together.

Rub the extra virgin olive oil over the chicken skin. Pour the olive oil into a roasting tin and put the chicken in the tin, breast up. Place the second sprig of rosemary on top.

Transfer to the oven and roast for 1 hour, turning the chicken and basting with the tin juices every 15 minutes.

Put the chicken on a warm serving plate and discard the rosemary sprig. Spoon off the fat from the roasting tin and place it over high heat on the stovetop. Add the chicken stock and deglaze the pan. Boil until reduced and thickened. Taste for salt and pepper, then pour into a sauceboat to accompany the chicken. Serve with roast rosemary potatoes.

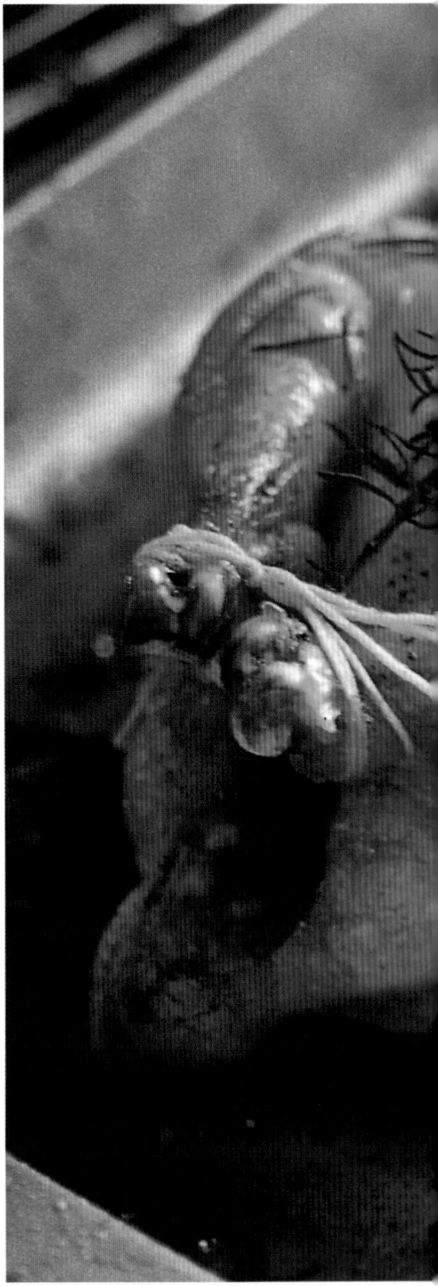

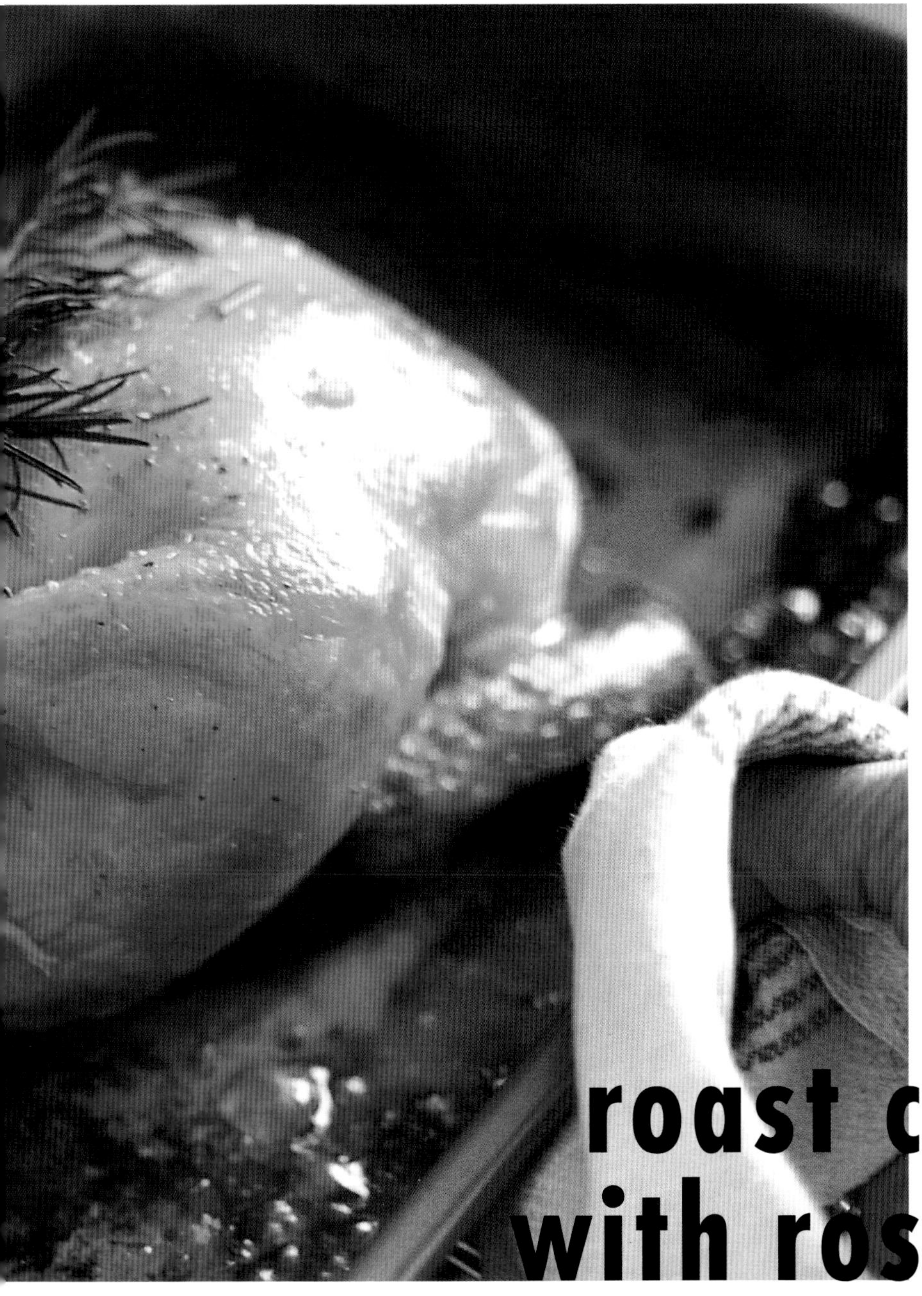

roast chicken with rosemary

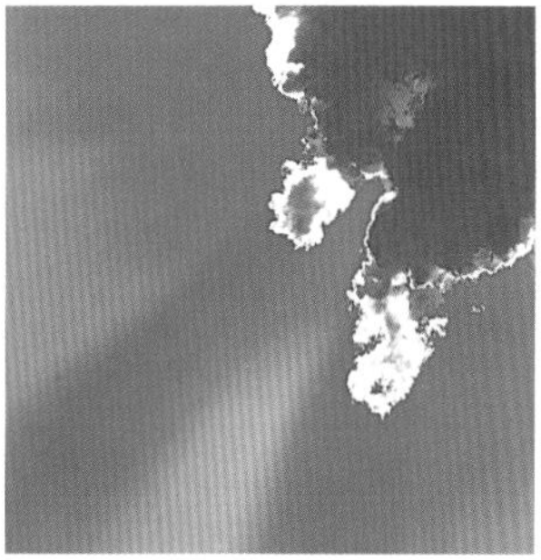

venison casserole

1 sprig of rosemary
1 large onion
1 garlic clove
80 g (3 oz) prosciutto
100 g (3½ oz) butter
1 kg (2 lb 4 oz) venison, cut into large cubes
1 litre (4 cups) beef stock
80 ml (⅓ cup) red wine vinegar
80 ml (⅓ cup) robust red wine
2 cloves
4 juniper berries
pinch of allspice
1 bay leaf
3 tablespoons plain (all-purpose) flour
2 tablespoons dry Marsala or brandy
1½ teaspoons grated lemon zest
1½ tablespoons finely chopped parsley

Serves 4

Strip the leaves off the rosemary and chop them finely with the onion, garlic and prosciutto. Heat half the butter in a large heavy saucepan with a lid. Add the chopped mixture and soften over moderately low heat for 5 minutes. Season with pepper. Increase the heat, add the venison and cook for 10 minutes, or until brown on all sides.

Put the stock in another saucepan and bring to the boil, then reduce the heat and keep at a low simmer.

Increase the heat under the venison, add the vinegar and cook until the liquid becomes thick and syrupy. Pour in the red wine. When that becomes syrupy, stir in half of the simmering stock. Add the cloves, juniper berries, allspice and bay leaf and cover the pan. Simmer for 1 hour, stirring once or twice and adding a little hot water if necessary to maintain the liquid level.

Meanwhile, melt the remaining butter in a saucepan. Stir in the flour and cook over moderately low heat for 1 minute. Slowly stir in the remaining stock and cook until the sauce thickens slightly.

Stir the sauce into the venison casserole, then add the Marsala. Uncover the pan and simmer for another 20 minutes. Taste for salt and pepper. Mix together the lemon zest and parsley and sprinkle over the top before serving.

1 x 1.5 kg (3 lb 5 oz) piece of beef, such as top rump or silverside
60 g (2¼ oz) pork fat, cut into small thin pieces
30 g (1 oz) butter
3 tablespoons olive oil
pinch of cayenne pepper
2 garlic cloves, finely chopped
2 onions, finely chopped
2 carrots, finely chopped
1 celery stalk, finely chopped
½ red capsicum (pepper), finely chopped
3 leeks, sliced
185 ml (¾ cup) red wine
1 tablespoon tomato paste (purée)
375 ml (1½ cups) beef stock
185 ml (¾ cup) tomato passata
8 basil leaves, torn into pieces
½ teaspoon finely chopped oregano leaves, or ¼ teaspoon dried oregano
2 tablespoons finely chopped parsley
60 ml (¼ cup) thick (double) cream

Serves 6

Make deep incisions all over the beef with the point of a sharp knife, then push a piece of pork fat into each incision.

Heat the butter and olive oil in a large casserole and brown the beef for 10–12 minutes, until it is browned all over. Season with salt and add the cayenne, garlic, onion, carrot, celery, pepper and leek. Cook over moderate heat for 10 minutes, until the vegetables are lightly browned.

Increase the heat, add the wine and boil until it has evaporated. Stir in the tomato paste, then add the stock. Simmer for 30 minutes. Add the passata, basil and oregano and season with pepper. Cover the casserole and cook for about 1 hour, or until the beef is tender.

Remove the beef from the casserole and allow it to rest for 10 minutes before carving. Taste the sauce for salt and pepper and stir in the parsley and cream.

beef cooked in ragù

ORISCERIA
PROVENZALE

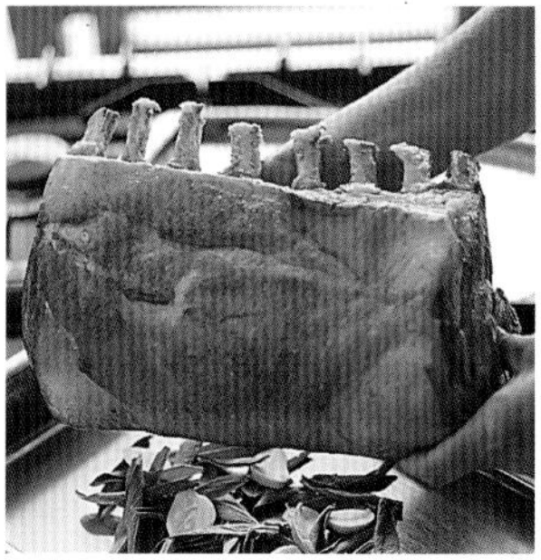

pork braised in milk

1 x 2.25 kg (5 lb) pork loin, chined (bone loosened) and skinned
60 ml (¼ cup) olive oil
4 garlic cloves, cut in half lengthways
15 g (½ oz) sage or rosemary leaves
1 litre (4 cups) milk
grated zest of 2 lemons
juice of 1 lemon

Serves 6

Preheat the oven to 200°C (400°F/Gas 6). Prepare the pork by trimming the fat to leave just a thin layer. The bone and fat keeps the pork moist.

Heat the olive oil in a large roasting tin. Add the pork and brown the meat on all sides. Remove the pork and pour away the fat from the roasting tin. Add the garlic and sage to the tin and place the pork on top of them. Season with salt and pepper and pour the milk over the pork. Return to the heat and bring just to the boil. Remove the tin from the heat again, add the lemon zest and drizzle with the lemon juice.

Transfer to the oven and roast for about 20 minutes. Reduce the temperature to 150°C (300°F/Gas 2) and cook for another 1–1¼ hours, depending on the thickness of the meat. If necessary, add a little more milk every so often, to keep the meat roasting in liquid. Baste the meat with the juices every 30 minutes. Do not cover, so that the juices reduce and the fat on the pork becomes crisp.

To test if the pork is cooked, poke a skewer into the middle of the meat, count to ten and pull it out. Touch it on the inside of your wrist and, if it feels hot, the meat is cooked through. Leave the meat to rest for 10 minutes before carving.

Strain the sauce if you like (you don't need to, but it may look curdled) and serve with the meat. Delicious served with braised fennel, cavolo nero or roasted vegetables.

185 ml (¾ cup) olive oil
1 onion, finely chopped
100 g (⅔ cup) pine nuts, roughly chopped
3 garlic cloves, crushed
40 g (1½ oz) parsley, roughly chopped
5 g (⅛ oz) basil or rosemary, roughly chopped
2 teaspoons fennel seeds, ground
50 g (⅔ cup) fresh breadcrumbs
250 g (1 cup) ricotta cheese
25 g (¼ cup) grated Parmesan cheese
grated zest of 1 large lemon
1 egg
500 g (1 lb 2 oz) minced (ground) pork or beef

SAUCE
800 g (1 lb 12 oz) tomatoes or 2 x 400 g (14 oz) tins tomatoes
125 ml (½ cup) red wine

Serves 4

Heat half the olive oil in a saucepan and cook the onion and pine nuts until the onion is soft and the pine nuts are light golden brown. Add the garlic and cook for a few minutes more, then set aside to cool.

Put the herbs, fennel seeds, breadcrumbs, ricotta, Parmesan, lemon zest and egg in a bowl and add the mince. Add the cooled onion and pine nuts, season with salt and pepper and mix briefly until all the ingredients are combined. Test for correct seasoning by frying one small meatball and tasting for flavour. Leave the mixture to rest in the fridge for at least 30 minutes or overnight.

To make the meatballs, roll about 50 g (1¾ oz) of mixture into a ball about the size of a walnut, then flatten slightly to make it easier to cook on both sides. Repeat with the rest of the mixture.

Heat the remaining olive oil in a large saucepan and fry the meatballs until golden brown on both sides. If necessary, cook them in two batches to prevent overcrowding the pan. Make sure there is enough oil to prevent the meatballs sticking to the base of the saucepan. Remove all the meatballs from the pan.

To make the sauce, if you are using fresh tomatoes, score a cross in the top of each one, plunge them into boiling water for 20 seconds, then drain and peel the skin away from the cross. Finely chop the flesh. Add the tomato and wine to the saucepan, season with salt and pepper and simmer for 5 minutes. Gently add the meatballs to the sauce and reduce the heat to a gentle simmer. Cover the saucepan and cook for another 10 minutes. Leave for 10 minutes before serving.

italian meatballs with tomato sauce

roast lamb

2 sprigs of rosemary
3 garlic cloves
75 g (2½ oz) pancetta
1 x 2 kg (4 lb 8 oz) leg of lamb, shank bone cut off just above the joint and trimmed of excess fat
1 large onion, cut into 4 thick slices
125 ml (½ cup) olive oil
375 ml (1½ cups) dry white wine

Serves 4

Preheat the oven to 230°C (450°F/Gas 8).

Strip the leaves off the rosemary sprigs and chop with the garlic and pancetta until fine and paste-like (a food processor works well for this). Season with a little salt and plenty of pepper.

With the point of a sharp knife, make incisions about 1 cm (½ inch) deep all over the lamb. Rub the rosemary filling over the surface of the lamb, pressing it into the incisions.

Put the onion slices in the centre of a roasting tin. Place the lamb on top and gently pour the olive oil over it. Roast for 15 minutes. Reduce the temperature to 180°C (350°F/Gas 4) and pour in 250 ml (1 cup) of the wine. Roast for 1 hour for medium-rare, or longer if you prefer. Baste a couple of times and add a little water if the juices start to burn in the tin. Transfer the lamb to a carving platter and leave to rest for 10 minutes.

Discard the onion and spoon off the excess fat from the tin. Place the tin over high heat on the stovetop, pour in the remaining wine and cook for 3–4 minutes, or until the sauce reduces and slightly thickens. Taste for seasoning. Slice the lamb and serve on a warm serving platter with the sauce spooned over the top.

850 g (1 lb 14 oz) Italian sausages
600 g (1 lb 5 oz) broccoli, cut into florets
1 teaspoon olive oil
2 French shallots, finely chopped
3 garlic cloves, crushed
¼ red chilli, finely chopped
125 ml (½ cup) chicken stock
1 tablespoon lemon juice
6 pitted black olives

Serves 4

Prick the sausages several times, then place them in a single layer in a deep non-stick frying pan and add cold water to a depth of 1.5 cm (⅝ inch). Bring to the boil, then reduce the heat and simmer for 20 minutes. Turn the sausages from time to time and add a little extra water should it evaporate too quickly—when the sausages are cooked, all the water will have evaporated, leaving just a little sausage fat in the pan.

Meanwhile, bring a large saucepan of water to the boil. Add the broccoli with a teaspoon of salt. Simmer for 4–5 minutes, or until the florets are barely tender. Drain and set aside.

Add the oil to the frying pan and evenly brown the sausages. Push the sausages to one side and add the shallots, garlic and chilli to the pan. Cook over low heat for 3–4 minutes, stirring from time to time. Add the stock and lemon juice, increase the heat and cook until reduced by half. Add the broccoli and olives, spoon the sauce over the broccoli and serve when it has heated through.

sausages with broccoli

salami & prosciutto... The Italians have turned their humble pig into a breathtaking array of deliciously sweet cured and cooked hams, pancetta, salami and sausages. Nowhere more than in the work of the *artigiani norcini*, artisan pork butchers, do you see the still close relationship in Italy between food and locality, hunting and eating.

All Italian homes used to raise a pig for the table—in rural areas they still do—and *norcini* travelled throughout the country during the butchering and curing season offering their services. Today, *norcineria* are butchers that specialize in pork and boar and their pig-shaped sign hung above a doorway guarantees local specialities, with the best labelled '*nostrano*', our own.

Many of Italy's famous salami are now mass-produced, but there are still countless varieties made to traditional local recipes. Southern salami are intense and spicy, like *Salame di Napoli,* flavoured with pepper, while the delicious salami of Central Italy include the *finocchiona,* a Tuscan salami speckled with the wild fennel seeds of the region, and Umbria's *salsiccia al tartufo,* the unusual pairing of pork and local black truffles. *Salame felino* from Parma is perhaps Italy's most refined salami—finely minced with a sweet taste. Other salami are made from wild boar or coarsely cut pork in a *cacciatore,* or hunter-style. Gnarled and uneven, they were traditionally made to be carried during hunting trips, carved into chunks with a sharp knife.

In the North, Parma ham, carved from magnificent hind legs of cured pork, is another local product shaped by its environment. The pure air of the Alta val Parma is used to wind-dry the pork to create the regal *prosciutto crudo,* raw ham. After a year, the final product, if it passes stringent tests, is proudly stamped with the crown of the Duke of Parma to signify its birthplace.

san nicola
prosciuttificio del sole

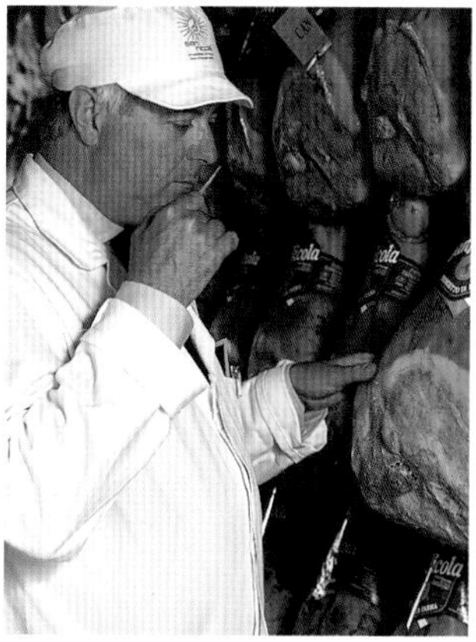

PANINI A PIACERE
COGLIONI DI MULO
AMARO AL TARTUFO £10000
VISA

eggplant parmigiana

1.5 kg (3 lb 5 oz) eggplants (aubergines)
plain (all-purpose) flour
350 ml (1⅓ cups) olive oil
500 ml (2 cups) tomato passata
2 tablespoons roughly torn basil leaves
250 g (1⅔ cups) grated mozzarella cheese
100 g (1 cup) grated Parmesan cheese

Serves 8

Thinly slice the eggplants lengthways. Layer the slices in a large colander, sprinkling salt between each layer. Leave for 1 hour to extract the bitter juices. Rinse and pat the slices dry on both sides with paper towels. Coat the eggplant slices lightly with flour.

Preheat the oven to 180°C (350°F/Gas 4) and grease a 32 x 20 cm (13 x 8 inch) shallow casserole or baking tray.

Heat 125 ml (½ cup) of the olive oil in a large frying pan. Quickly fry the eggplant in batches over moderately high heat until crisp and golden on both sides. Add more olive oil as needed, and drain well on paper towels as you remove each batch from the pan.

Make a slightly overlapping layer of eggplant slices over the base of the dish. Season with pepper. Spoon 4 tablespoons of passata over the eggplant and scatter a few pieces of basil on top. Sprinkle with some mozzarella, followed by some Parmesan. Continue with this layering until you have used up all the ingredients. Bake for 30 minutes. Remove from the oven and allow to cool for 30 minutes before serving.

350 g (12 oz) dried borlotti beans
440 ml (1¾ cups) dry red wine
1 small onion, finely chopped
3 cloves
125 ml (½ cup) olive oil
1 sprig of rosemary
3 garlic cloves, crushed
pinch of chilli flakes
3 tablespoons chopped parsley

Serves 6

Soak the beans in cold water overnight, then drain. Place in a large saucepan and add the wine, onion, cloves, half the olive oil and 875 ml (3½ cups) water. Cover and bring to the boil. Reduce the heat, remove the lid and simmer for 1 hour.

Heat the remaining oil in a small saucepan. Strip the leaves off the rosemary sprig and chop finely. Place in the oil with the garlic and chilli and cook for 1 minute. Add to the beans and simmer for 30 minutes to 1 hour, until the beans are tender.

Drain the beans, reserving the cooking liquid. Return the cooking liquid to the pan and simmer until it thickens. Season. Return the beans to the pan and simmer for another 5 minutes. Stir in the parsley and cool for 15 minutes before serving.

braised borlotti beans

potato and pumpkin gratin

450 g (1 lb) potatoes, thinly sliced
leaves from 3 large sprigs of thyme or rosemary, finely chopped
700 g (1 lb 9 oz) pumpkin (squash), thinly sliced
1 large garlic clove, crushed
500 ml (2 cups) thick (double) cream

Serves 4

Preheat the oven to 180°C (375°F/Gas 4). Lightly grease a 25 x 23 cm (10 x 9 inch) gratin dish with a little butter. Arrange a layer of potato in the dish, season with salt, pepper and herbs, then top with a layer of pumpkin. Continue the layers, finishing with pumpkin. Mix the garlic with the cream and pour over the top. Cover the dish with buttered foil and bake in the oven for about 45 minutes.

Test to see if the gratin is cooked by inserting a knife into the centre. If the slices seem soft, it is cooked. Remove the foil and increase the oven temperature to 190°C (375°F/Gas 5). Cook for another 15 minutes, or until there is a good brown crust on top. Leave to rest for at least 10 minutes before serving. Delicious served with grilled (broiled) meats or on its own with just a green salad.

POLENTA
1 tablespoon salt
300 g (2 cups) coarse-grain polenta
75 g (2½ oz) butter

TOMATO SAUCE
3 tablespoons olive oil
2 garlic cloves, thinly sliced
15 g (½ oz) rosemary or thyme, roughly chopped
800 g (1 lb 12 oz) tin tomatoes
200 g (7 oz) Gorgonzola cheese, cubed
250 g (9 oz) Taleggio cheese, cubed
250 g (1¼ cups) mascarpone cheese
100 g (1 cup) grated Parmesan cheese

Serves 6

Bring 1.5 litres (6 cups) water to the boil in a heavy-based saucepan and add the salt. Add the polenta in a gentle stream, whisking or stirring vigorously as you pour it in. Reduce the heat immediately so that the water is simmering. Stir continuously for the first 30 seconds to avoid any lumps—the more you stir, the better the texture will be. Once you have stirred well at the beginning you can leave the polenta to bubble away, stirring it every few minutes to prevent it sticking. Cook for 40 minutes. Add the butter and mix.

Pour the polenta into a shallow casserole or baking dish about 5 cm (2 inches) deep (you want the polenta to come no more than halfway up the side of the dish). Leave to cool completely.

To make the tomato sauce, heat the olive oil in a saucepan and cook the garlic gently until light brown. Add half the rosemary or thyme and then the tomatoes. Season with salt and pepper and cook gently, stirring occasionally, until reduced to a thick tomato sauce.

Preheat the oven to 180°C (350°F/Gas 4). Turn the polenta out of the dish and onto a board, then slice it horizontally in two. Pour half the tomato sauce into the bottom of the empty dish. Place the bottom slice of the polenta on top of the sauce and season. Scatter the Gorgonzola and Taleggio over the top. Dot the mascarpone over the polenta with a teaspoon, and sprinkle with half the Parmesan and the remaining herbs. Put the other layer of polenta on top and pour over the remaining tomato sauce. Sprinkle with the remaining Parmesan and bake for 30 minutes. Leave to rest for 10 minutes before serving with a simple rocket (arugula) salad.

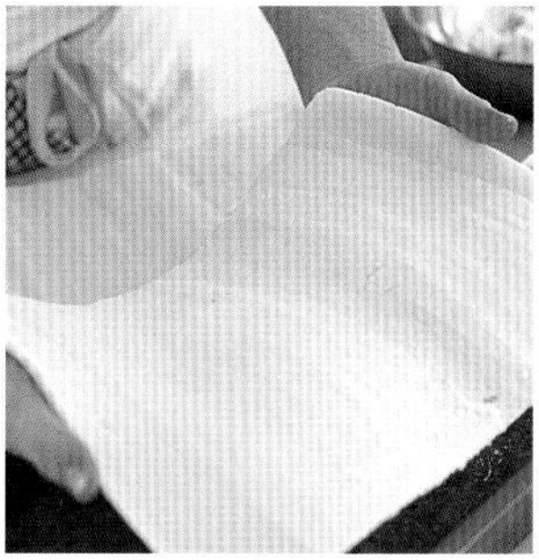

baked polenta with four cheeses

a little taste of...

The Italian bar is really a coffee bar rather than a drinking bar, but in a country where drinking is never separated from the daily routines of life, it does of course serve alcohol as well. From early in the morning, customers drop by for a *caffé corretto,* a coffee laced with grappa or brandy, and after a hard morning, many order a shot of liqueur alongside their espresso. An essential part of every neighbourhood, bars are busy from early in the morning serving breakfast cappuccinos, and they are the place for a simple lunch of hot panini or a mid-afternoon gelato stop. In the evening a *birra* (beer) or a tall elegant Campari is always accompanied by a little food chosen from the selection on the bar. Perhaps a plate of olives, tiny hot balls of arancini, with their melting insides of mozzarella, or crostini, topped with crushed olives, sweet tomatoes or capsicums (peppers). Regulars stand at the bar, the cheapest option, but on a hot evening, tables of friends and family spill out noisily onto the streets.

...al bar

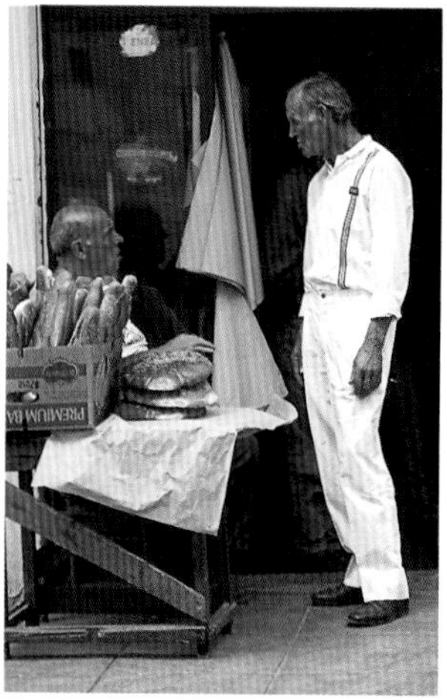

bruschetta

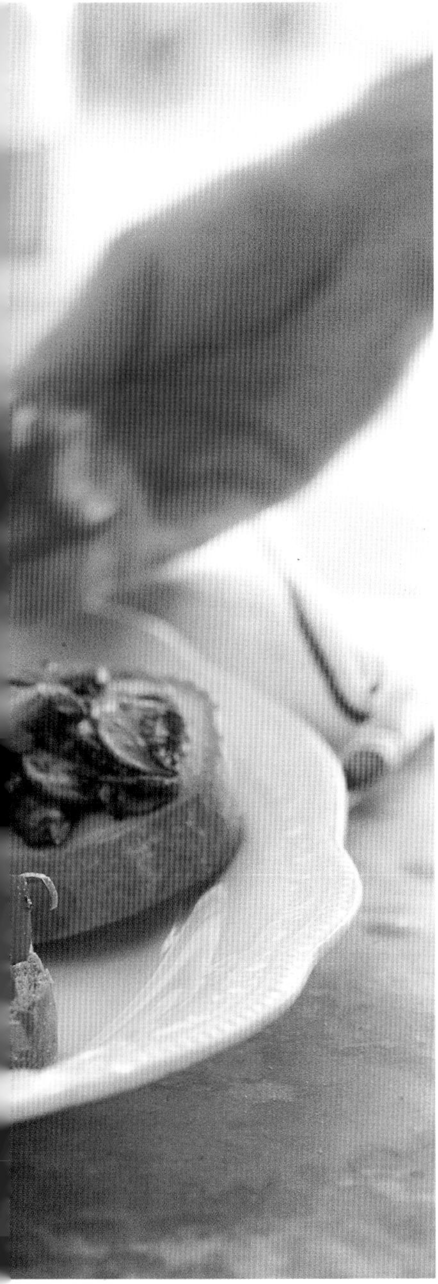

4 large slices of 'country-style' bread, such as ciabatta
1 garlic clove, cut in half
drizzle of extra virgin olive oil

Makes 4

Toast, chargrill or grill (broil) the bread until it is crisp. Rub the cut edge of the garlic over both sides of each bread slice and drizzle oil over each slice.

TOMATO AND BASIL BRUSCHETTA

4 ripe tomatoes
1 tablespoon shredded basil
4 pieces basic bruschetta

Serves 4

Roughly chop the tomatoes and mix with the basil. Season well and pile onto the bruschetta.

WILD MUSHROOM BRUSCHETTA

2 tablespoons olive oil
400 g (14 oz) selection of wild mushrooms, particularly fresh porcini, sliced if large, or chestnut mushrooms
2 garlic cloves, crushed
1 heaped tablespoon chopped thyme
4 pieces basic bruschetta

Serves 4

Heat the olive oil in a large saucepan or frying pan. When the oil is hot, add just enough mushrooms to cover the base of the pan and cook over high heat, stirring frequently. Season with salt and pepper. (Sometimes the mushrooms can become watery when cooked. Continue cooking until all the liquid has evaporated.)

Add the crushed garlic and thyme and cook for another minute. Remove from the pan and repeat with the remaining mushrooms. Spoon over the bruschetta and serve immediately.

CROSTINI
2 day-old ciabatta or 1 day-old pugliese, thinly sliced and cut into quarters
185 ml (3/4 cup) extra virgin olive oil

Makes 50

RED CAPSICUM
3 tablespoons olive oil
1 onion, finely chopped
2 red capsicums (peppers), thinly sliced
2 garlic cloves, crushed
1 tablespoon capers, drained and chopped
2 tablespoons balsamic vinegar
1 tablespoon roughly chopped flat-leaf parsley

CHICKEN LIVER
3 tablespoons chicken liver pâté

TAPENADE
1 quantity tapenade (page 250)

To make the crostini, preheat the oven to 180°C (350°F/Gas 4). Drizzle the bread with olive oil over both sides, then lightly toast in the oven until just crisp. The crostini will keep in an airtight container for a couple of days.

To make the red capsicum crostini, heat the olive oil in a frying pan and cook the onion for a few minutes until soft. Add the capsicums and cook for another 15 minutes, stirring frequently. Season. Add the garlic and cook for another minute. Add the capers and vinegar and simmer gently for a few minutes to reduce the liquid. Add the chopped parsley just before spreading onto crostini.

To make the chicken liver crostini and the tapenade crostini, spread some pâté and tapenade on crostini.

crostini

campari & cinzano

Italians like to enjoy their evenings and in a country where dinner rarely starts before eight—in the South, the *primo piatti* can appear as late as ten—there is plenty of time to enjoy an *aperitivo*. Indeed, by sunset the whole of Italy seems to be out on the streets taking part in the national evening stroll, *la passegiata*. The bars are filled with grappa-drinking regulars holding court at the counter, while friends on the *terazzo* sip their drinks and snack on tapenade crostini or tiny pizzettes chosen from the laden bar. Here, as always, the Italians don't separate their drink and food—the two are there to be enjoyed together.

There are some wonderful *aperitivi* to choose from. Campari from Milan, with its bitter taste and vivid red hue, is usually drunk unadorned—poured over ice and sometimes topped up with soda or juice. Cinzano and Martini are vermouths made in Turin, sweet or dry, they are served with a twist of lemon or orange. There are also local *aperitivi* to rival the big names. Limoncello, made by infusing lemon zest in alcohol, is the drink in the glamorous towns along the citrus-producing Amalfi coast, while in the Veneto, sparkling *prosecco* is mixed with peach juice in a bellini. Local grappa, Italian firewater, is another potent *aperitivo*.

suppli

3 tablespoons butter
1 small onion, finely chopped
1.5 litres (6 cups) chicken stock
440 g (2 cups) risotto rice (vialone nano, arborio or carnaroli)
75 g (3/4 cup) grated Parmesan cheese
2 eggs, beaten
9 basil leaves, torn in half
150 g (5 1/2 oz) mozzarella cheese, cut into 18 cubes (about 1.5 cm / 5/8 inch square)
150 g (1 1/2 cups) dried breadcrumbs
oil for deep-frying

Serves 6

Melt the butter in a large saucepan. Add the onion and cook over low heat for 3–4 minutes, until softened but not browned. Heat the stock to simmering point in another saucepan.

Add the rice to the onion and cook, stirring, for 1 minute to seal the rice. Add several ladles of the hot stock, stirring continuously so that the rice cooks evenly. Keep adding enough stock to just cover the rice, stirring frequently. Continue in this way for about 20 minutes, or until the rice is creamy on the outside but still *al dente*.

Remove from the heat and stir in the Parmesan and eggs. Season with salt and pepper. Spread out on a large baking tray to cool completely.

Divide the rice into 18 portions. Take one portion in the palm of your hand and put a piece of basil and a cube of mozzarella in the centre. Fold the rice over to encase the cheese and, at the same time, mould the croquette into an egg shape. Roll the croquette in breadcrumbs and place on a baking tray.

Heat enough oil in a deep-fat fryer or deep frying pan to fully cover the croquettes. Heat the oil to 180°C (350°F), or until a piece of bread fries golden brown in 15 seconds when dropped in the oil. Deep-fry the suppli in batches, without crowding, for about 4 minutes, or until evenly golden brown. Drain on paper towels and serve at once, as they are or with a fresh tomato sauce (page 251).

175 g (6 oz) broad beans, fresh or frozen
1 onion
400 g (14 oz) tin artichoke hearts, drained
3 tablespoons olive oil
6 eggs
2 tablespoons chopped parsley
45 g (½ cup) grated pecorino cheese
pinch of nutmeg

Serves 4

Bring a small saucepan of water to the boil and add a large pinch of salt and the broad beans. Boil for 2 minutes, then drain and rinse under cold water. Peel off the skins from the beans.

Halve the onion and slice thinly. Cut the artichoke hearts from bottom to top into slices about 5 mm (¼ inch) wide. Discard any slices that contain the tough central choke.

Heat the oil in a 30 cm (12 inch) frying pan and fry the onion over low heat for 6–8 minutes, without allowing it to brown. Add the artichoke slices and cook for 1–2 minutes. Stir in the broad beans.

Preheat the grill (broiler). Lightly beat together the eggs, parsley, pecorino and nutmeg and season well with salt and pepper. Pour into the frying pan and cook over low heat until three-quarters set, shaking the pan often to stop the frittata sticking.

Finish the top off under the grill and leave to cool before serving in wedges.

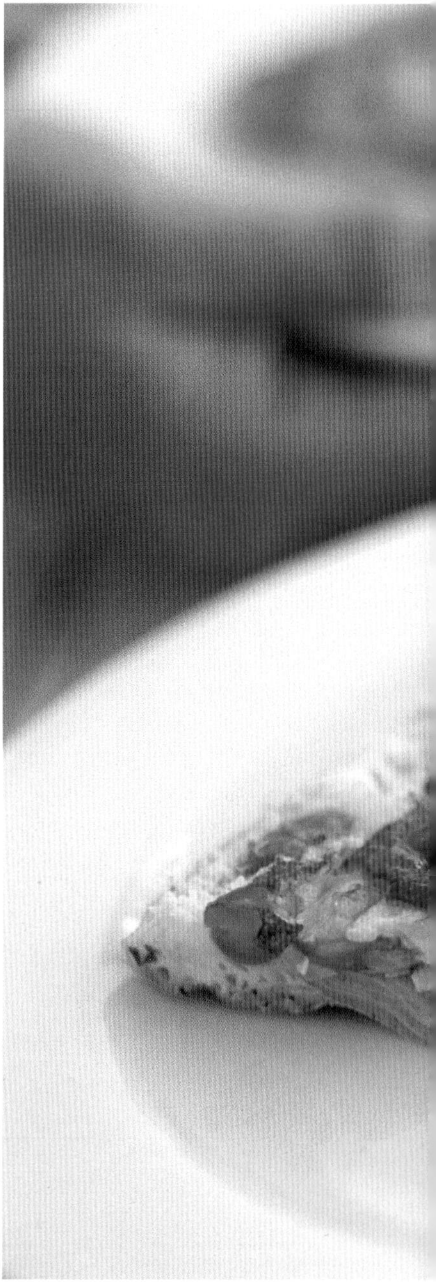

artichoke frittata

a little taste of...

Gelaterie are the treasure boxes of Italy, the best often tucked away, serving a loyal local clientele out of a tiny mobile van, a hole-in-the-wall stall in the daily market or a simple shop in the suburbs. But behind these plain façades lie magical displays of sometimes as many as 70 delicious gelati, granite and sorbetti, with an ever changing selection of flavours reflecting the seasons' harvests and the proprietor's latest exotic combinations. Gelaterie serve scoops of their ice cream in a *cono* (cone) or *coppetta* (tub) and the Italians love both the thick, rich *crema* (creamy) gelati and the pure *frutta* (fruit) ices. Some of the most popular varieties are really frozen desserts, often unbelievably imaginative, and a gelateria can become famous for just one flavour, perhaps Sicilian *cassata,* speckled with pistachio or candied fruit, *limoncini alla crema* (candied lemon) or *tartufo* (vanilla covered in bittersweet chocolate). Always popular, gelaterie open long hours, often serving into the night when, for many families, they are the all-important highlight of the *passegiata,* their evening stroll.

...gelateria

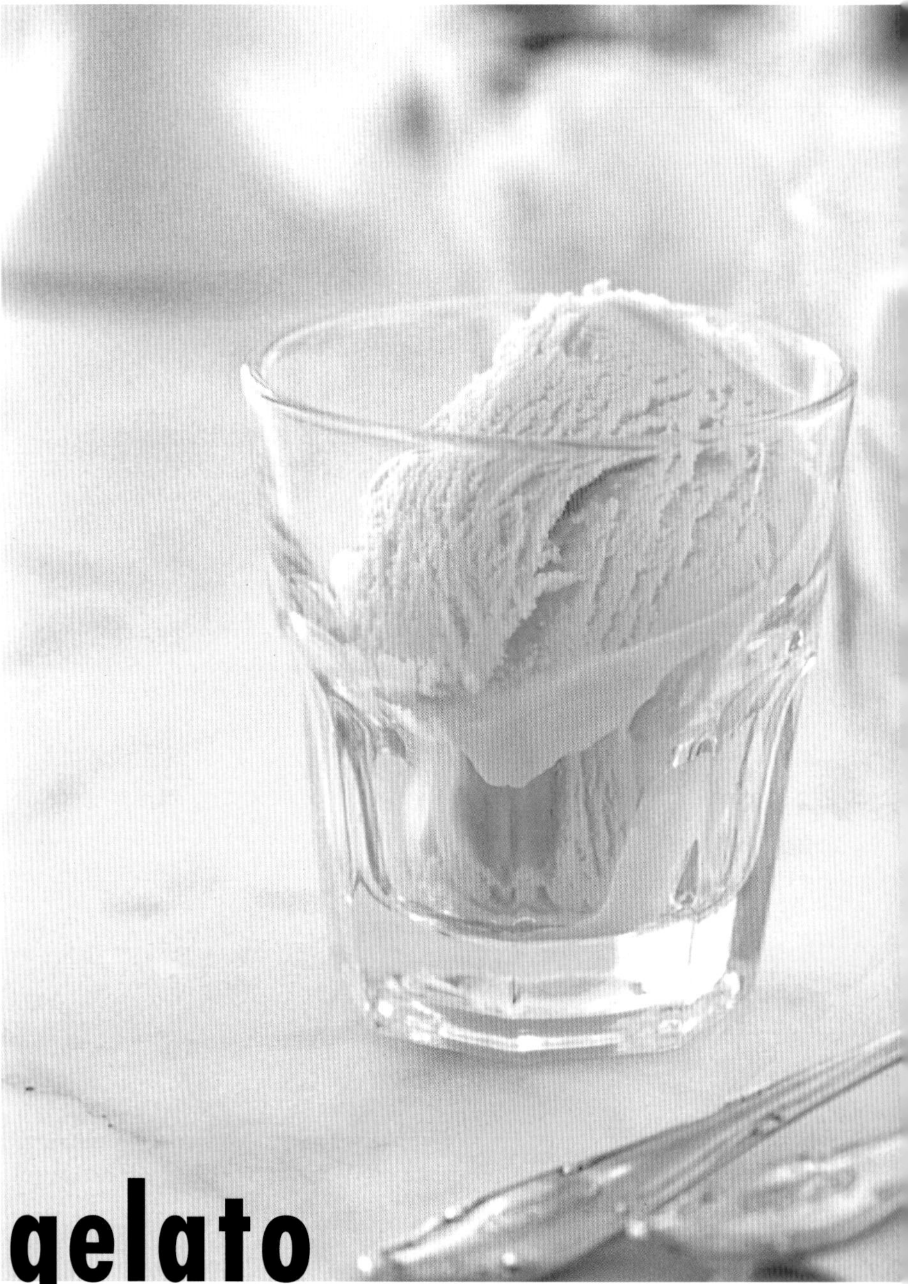

lemon gelato

5 egg yolks
110 g (½ cup) sugar
500 ml (2 cups) milk
2 tablespoons grated lemon zest
185 ml (¾ cup) lemon juice
3 tablespoons thick (double) cream

Serves 6

Whisk the egg yolks and half the sugar together until pale and creamy. Place the milk, lemon zest and remaining sugar in a saucepan and bring to the boil. Pour over the egg mixture and whisk to combine. Pour the custard back into the saucepan and cook over low heat, stirring continuously until the mixture is thick enough to coat the back of a wooden spoon—do not allow the custard to boil.

Strain the custard into a bowl, add the lemon juice and cream and then cool over ice. Churn in an ice-cream maker following the manufacturer's instructions. Alternatively, pour into a plastic freezer box, cover and freeze. Stir every 30 minutes with a whisk during freezing to break up the ice crystals and give a better texture. Keep in the freezer until ready to serve.

5 egg yolks
110 g (½ cup) sugar
500 ml (2 cups) milk
125 ml (½ cup) freshly made espresso
1 tablespoon Tia Maria

Serves 6

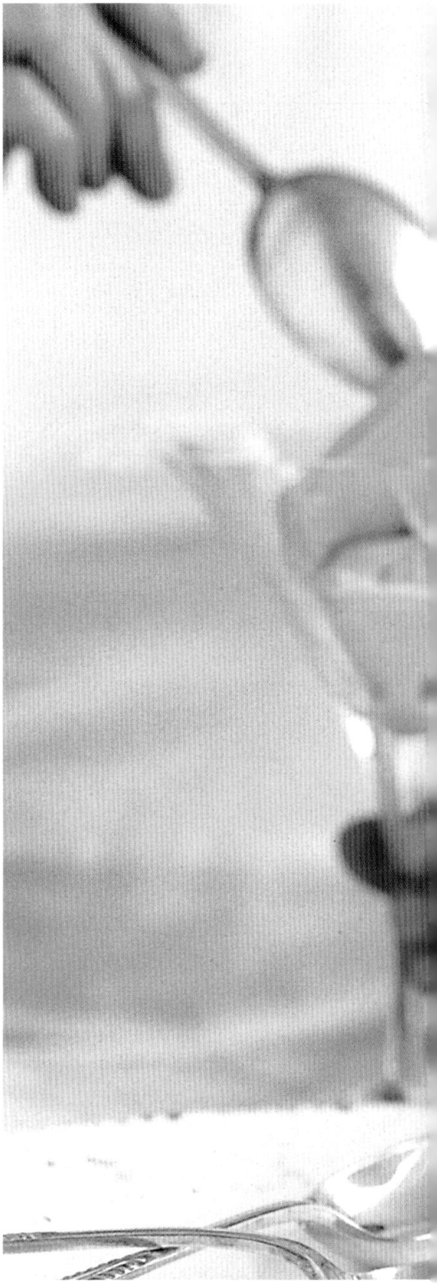

Whisk the egg yolks and half the sugar together until pale and creamy. Place the milk, coffee and remaining sugar in a saucepan and bring to the boil. Pour over the egg mixture and whisk to combine. Pour back into the saucepan and cook over low heat, stirring continuously until the mixture is thick enough to coat the back of a wooden spoon—do not allow the custard to boil.

Strain the custard into a bowl and cool over ice. Stir in the Tia Maria. Churn in an ice-cream maker following the manufacturer's instructions. Alternatively, pour into a plastic freezer box, cover and freeze. Stir every 30 minutes with a whisk during freezing to break up the ice crystals and give a better texture. Keep in the freezer until ready to serve.

coffee gelato

praline semifreddo

150 g (5½ oz) croccante (praline)
600 ml (2½ cups) thick (double) cream
2 eggs, separated
90 g (¾ cup) icing (confectioners') sugar
2 tablespoons Mandorla (almond-flavoured Marsala) or brandy

Serves 6

Finely crush the croccante in a food processor or with a rolling pin. Pour the cream into a large bowl and whisk until soft peaks form. Beat the egg yolks with a quarter of the icing sugar until pale. Whisk the egg whites in a clean dry glass bowl until stiff peaks form, then gradually add the rest of the icing sugar and whisk until glossy stiff peaks form. Gently fold the egg yolks into the cream, then fold in the egg whites. Fold in the almonds and Mandorla.

Line six 250 ml (1-cup) metal dariole moulds with two long strips of foil each. Spoon in the mixture, level the surface and tap each mould on the bench a few times. Cover the surface with more foil and freeze for at least 24 hours. To unmould, leave at room temperature for 5 minutes, then use the foil strips as handles to lift out the semifreddos. Serve with zabaione (page 239).

500 ml (2 cups) thick (double) cream
170 g (3/4 cup) caster (superfine) sugar
60 g (1/2 cup) cocoa powder
4 eggs, separated
3 tablespoons brandy
3 tablespoons icing (confectioners') sugar
150 g (5 1/2 oz) skinned hazelnuts, roughly chopped

Serves 10

Line a 1.5 litre (6-cup) loaf tin with two long strips of foil. Heat 185 ml (3/4 cup) of the cream in a small saucepan. Combine the caster sugar, cocoa powder and egg yolks in a bowl. Pour the hot cream on top and mix well. Pour back into the saucepan and cook over low heat, stirring continuously, until the mixture is thick enough to coat the back of a wooden spoon—do not allow the custard to boil. Stir in the brandy and remove from the heat. Cover the surface with plastic wrap and cool for 30 minutes.

Whip the egg whites in a clean dry glass bowl until stiff peaks form. Whip the remaining cream in a large bowl until soft peaks form. Add the icing sugar and continue whipping until stiff and glossy. Lightly fold the chocolate custard into the whipped cream, then fold in the egg whites. Gently fold through the hazelnuts. Spoon into the tin, smooth the surface and cover with foil. Freeze for at least 24 hours. Leave at room temperature for 5 minutes before serving in slices.

chocolate semifreddo

gelati & granite

The Italians make fantastic *sorbetti* and *granite*, water ices, and *gelati di crema*, ice creams. Every bar has a small selection, always including *cioccolato* (chocolate) and *nocciola* (hazelnut), the most basic flavours, while a *gelateria* will sell at least 20 varieties. The most spectacular are the deeply coloured fruit ices, which seem simply a frozen spoonful of the real thing, from wild blueberry, raspberry and fig to sweet Amalfi lemon and different shades of melon.

The best *gelati* are *produzione proprio*, made on the premises, with seasonal ingredients ranging from Sicilian blood oranges in the winter to ripe peaches in the heat of summer. The base of Italian ice cream is an egg custard

rather than cream, and this blends easily with fresh fruit juices, while Italian regulations prohibit anything except natural sweetness. The Italians also love more elaborate flavours, their *semifreddo*—frozen desserts—iced rice puddings, tiramisu and Marsala-soaked *zabaione*.

Granite are grainy water ices renowned all over Italy as a southern speciality. *Caffé granita* is made from a strong espresso and served ice-cold in cafés in the summer instead of coffee. *Granita di limone* is made from shaved ice, fresh citrus juice and a little syrup—though not too much or it won't freeze, and sold from tiny stalls in the noisy cities of the South to cool down a hot afternoon.

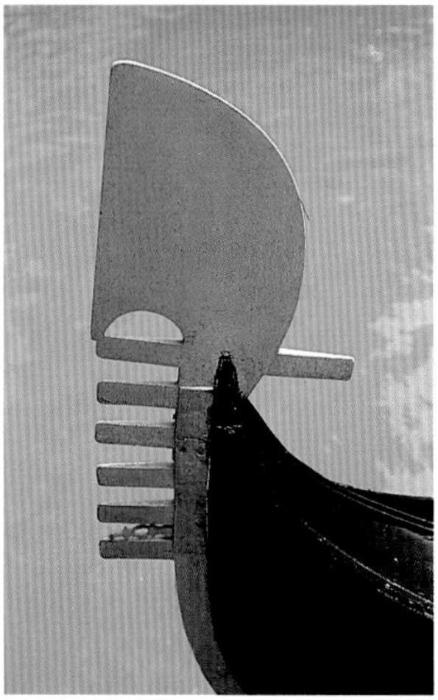

raspberry sorbet

115 g (½ cup) sugar
1 tablespoon liquid glucose or caster (superfine) sugar
¼ teaspoon lemon juice
200 g (7 oz) raspberries

Serves 4

Heat the sugar, glucose, lemon juice and 250 ml (1 cup) water in a small saucepan for 4 minutes, or until dissolved. Purée the raspberries in a blender or food processor, or by mashing with the back of a spoon, add the syrup and process until puréed. Pass through a nylon sieve to remove the seeds.

Churn in an ice-cream maker following the manufacturer's instructions. Alternatively, pour into a plastic freezer box, cover and freeze. Stir every 30 minutes with a whisk during freezing to break up the ice crystals and give a better texture. Keep in the freezer until ready to serve.

450 g (1 lb) watermelon, rind and seeds removed
1 tablespoon liquid glucose or caster (superfine) sugar
½ teaspoon lemon juice

Serves 4

Purée the watermelon in a blender or food processor, or chop it finely and push it through a metal sieve. Heat the glucose, lemon juice and 80 ml (⅓ cup) water in a small saucepan for 4 minutes, or until dissolved. Add the watermelon and stir well.

Pour into a plastic freezer box, cover and freeze. Stir every 30 minutes with a fork during freezing to break up the ice crystals and give a better texture. Keep in the freezer until ready to serve, then roughly fork to break up the ice crystals.

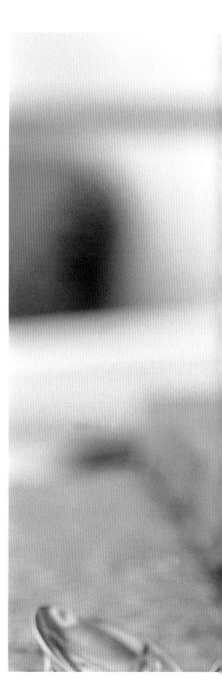

watermelon granita

tiramisu

5 eggs, separated
170 g (3/4 cup) caster (superfine) sugar
300 g (10½ oz) mascarpone cheese
250 ml (1 cup) cold strong coffee
3 tablespoons brandy or sweet Marsala
36 small sponge fingers
80 g (3 oz) dark chocolate, finely grated

Serves 4

Beat the egg yolks with the sugar until the sugar has dissolved and the mixture is light and fluffy and leaves a ribbon trail when dropped from the whisk. Add the mascarpone and beat until the mixture is smooth.

Whisk the egg whites in a clean dry glass bowl, using a wire whisk or hand beaters, until soft peaks form. Fold into the mascarpone mixture.

Pour the coffee into a shallow dish and add the brandy. Dip enough biscuits to cover the base of a 25 cm (10 inch) square dish into the coffee. The biscuits should be fairly well soaked but not so much so that they break up. Arrange the biscuits in one tightly packed layer in the base of the dish.

Spread half the mascarpone mixture over the layer of biscuits. Add another layer of soaked biscuits and then another layer of mascarpone, smoothing the top layer neatly. Dust with the grated chocolate to serve. The flavours will be better developed if you can make the tiramisu a few hours in advance or even the night before. If you have time to do this, don't dust with the chocolate, but cover with plastic wrap and chill. Dust with chocolate at the last minute or it will melt.

500 ml (2 cups) thick (double) cream
4 tablespoons caster (superfine) sugar
vanilla extract
3 sheets or 1¼ teaspoons gelatine
250 g (9 oz) fresh berries

Serves 4

Put the cream and sugar in a saucepan and stir over gentle heat until the sugar has dissolved. Bring to the boil, then simmer for 3 minutes, adding a few drops of vanilla extract to taste.

If you are using the gelatine sheets, soak in cold water until they are floppy, then squeeze out any excess water. Stir the sheets into the hot cream until they are completely dissolved. If you are using powdered gelatine, sprinkle it onto the hot cream in an even layer and leave it to sponge for a minute, then stir it into the cream until dissolved.

Pour the cream mixture into four 125 ml (½-cup) dariole moulds, cover each with a piece of plastic wrap and refrigerate until set.

Unmould the panna cotta by wrapping the moulds in a cloth dipped in hot water and tipping them gently onto individual plates. Serve with the fresh berries.

panna cotta

frappé granite brioc
LIMONE
LATTE DI MANDORLA
MENTA - L.2500 -
AMARENA -
PRODUZIONE ARTIGIANALE
Gelateria dei

Gelateria dei golosi
I GELATI DEL GIORNO
panna
after eight
pistacchio
gianduia
yogurth
caffè
fragola
cioccolato
limone
stracciatella
cocco
nocciola
banana
liquirizia
Crema Miele Noci
FRAPPÉ
golosi

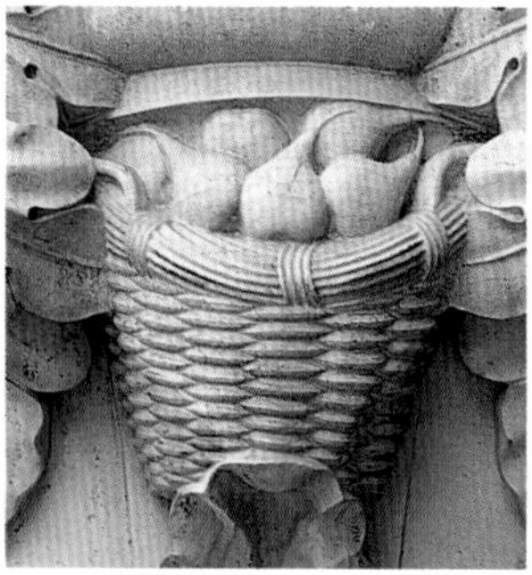

zabaione

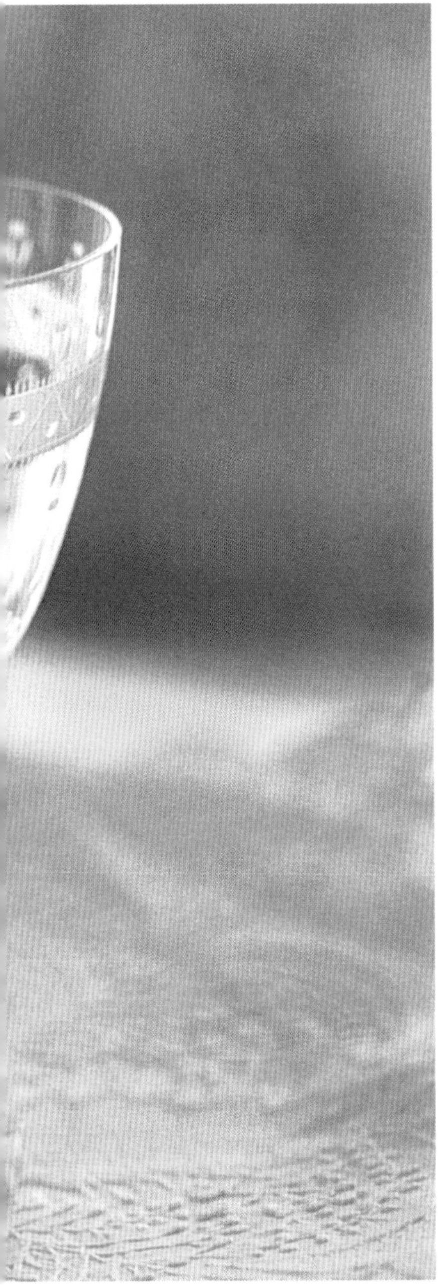

6 egg yolks
3 tablespoons caster (superfine) sugar
125 ml (½ cup) sweet Marsala
250 ml (1 cup) thick (double) cream

Serves 4

Whisk the egg yolks and sugar together in the top of a double boiler or in a heatproof bowl set over a saucepan of simmering water. When the mixture is tepid, pour in the Marsala and whisk the mixture for another 5 minutes, or until it has thickened.

Whip the cream until soft peaks form. Gently fold in the egg yolk mixture. Cover and refrigerate for 3–4 hours before serving.

400 g (14 oz) Madeira or pound cake
4 tablespoons sweet Marsala
350 g (12 oz) ricotta cheese
110 g (4 oz) caster (superfine) sugar
½ teaspoon vanilla extract
150 g (5½ oz) mixed candied fruit (orange, lemon, cherries, pineapple, apricot), chopped
50 g (1¾ oz) dark chocolate, chopped
green food colouring
200 g (7 oz) marzipan
2 tablespoons apricot jam
310 g (2½ cups) icing (confectioners') sugar

Makes one 20 cm (8 inch) cake

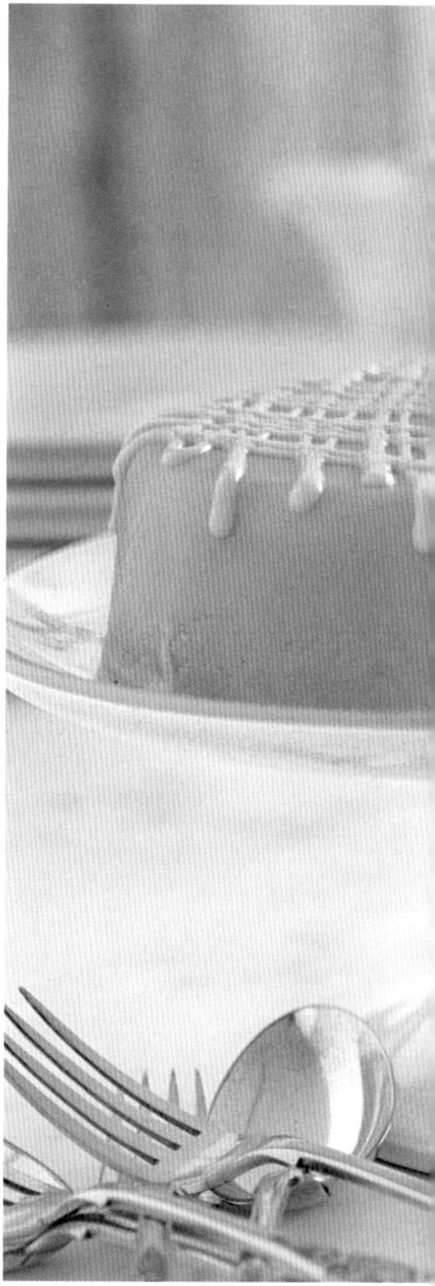

Line a 20 cm (8 inch) round cake tin with sloping sides (a moule à manqué would be perfect) with plastic wrap. Cut the cake into thin slices to line the tin, reserving enough pieces to cover the top at the end. Fit the slices of cake carefully into the tin, making sure there are no gaps. Sprinkle the Marsala over the cake in the tin.

Put the ricotta in a bowl and beat until smooth. Add the sugar and vanilla extract and mix well. Add the candied fruit and chocolate and mix well. Spoon into the mould, smooth the surface and then cover with the reserved slices of cake. Cover with plastic wrap and press the top down hard. Put the cassata in the fridge for at least two hours or preferably overnight, then unmould onto a plate.

Knead enough green food colouring into the marzipan to colour it light green. Roll out the marzipan in a circle until it is large enough to completely cover the cassata. Melt the jam in a saucepan with a tablespoon of water and brush over the cassata. Lift the marzipan over the top and trim it to fit around the edge.

Mix the icing sugar with a little hot water to make a smooth icing that will spread easily. Either pipe the icing onto the cassata in a decorative pattern, or drizzle it over the top in a crosshatch pattern.

cassata

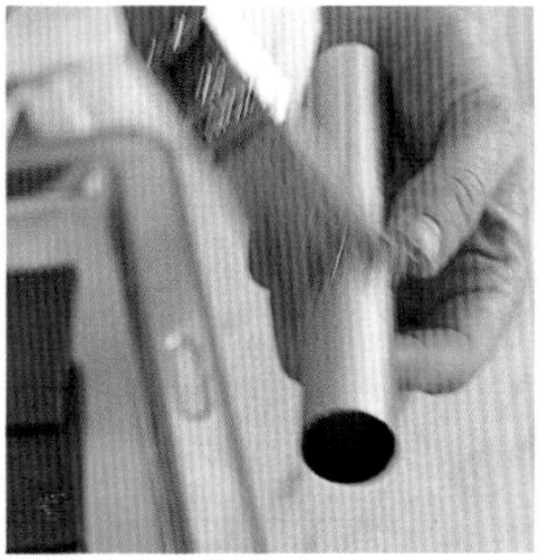

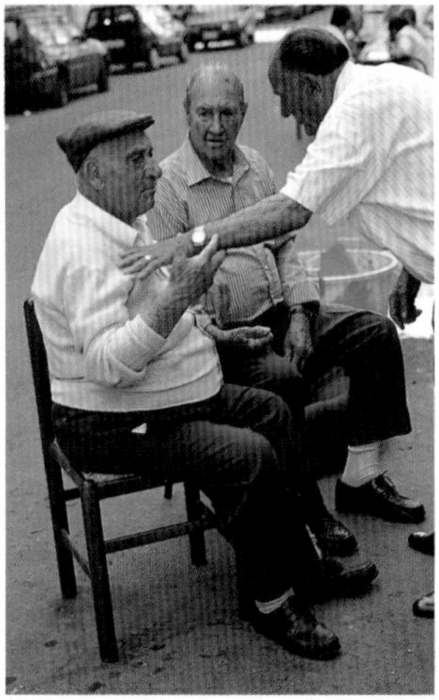

cannoli

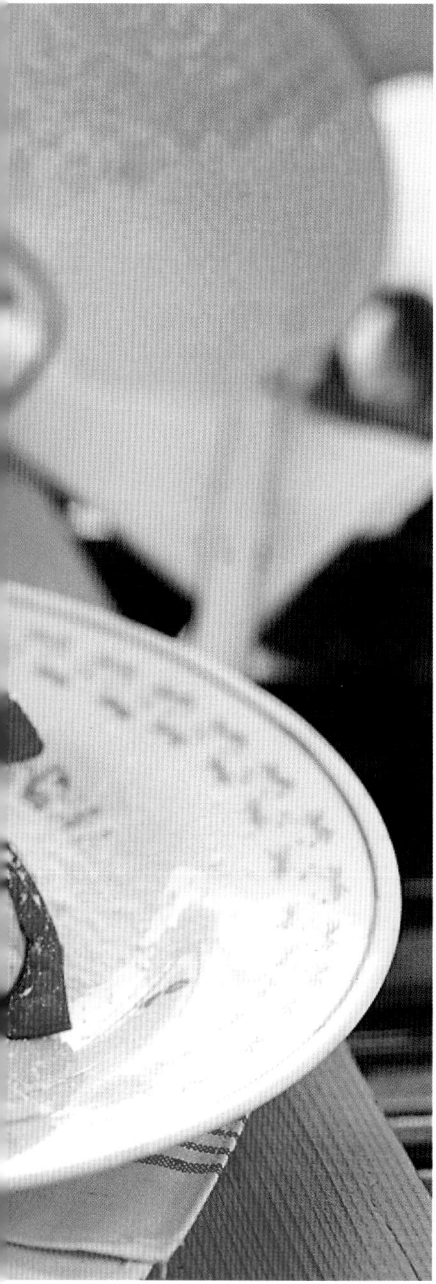

PASTRY
150 g (1¼ cups) plain (all-purpose) flour
2 teaspoons cocoa powder
1 teaspoon instant coffee powder
1 tablespoon caster (superfine) sugar
20 g (1 oz) unsalted butter, chilled and cut into small cubes
3 tablespoons dry white wine
1 teaspoon dry Marsala

1 egg, beaten
oil for deep-frying

FILLING
300 g (10½ oz) ricotta cheese
150 g (⅔ cup) caster (superfine) sugar
¼ teaspoon vanilla extract
½ teaspoon grated lemon zest
1 tablespoon candied peel, finely chopped
6 glacé cherries, chopped
15 g (½ oz) dark chocolate, grated
icing (confectioners') sugar

Serves 6

To make the pastry, mix the flour, cocoa powder, coffee powder and sugar in a bowl. Rub in the butter, then add the wine and Marsala and mix until the dough gathers in a loose clump. Transfer to a lightly floured surface and knead until smooth (the dough will be quite stiff). Chill in a plastic bag for 30 minutes.

Lightly dust the work surface with flour and roll the pastry out to about 32 x 24 cm (13 x 9 inch). Trim the edges, then cut the pastry into twelve 8 cm (3 inch) squares. Lightly oil the metal cannoli tubes (from speciality kitchen shops). Wrap a pastry square diagonally around each tube, securing the overlapping corners with beaten egg and pressing them firmly together.

Heat the oil in a deep-fat fryer or deep frying pan to about 180°C (350°F), or until a scrap of pastry dropped into the oil becomes crisp and golden, with a slightly blistered surface, in 15–20 seconds. If the oil starts to smoke it is too hot. Add the cannoli, a couple at a time, and deep-fry until golden and crisp. Remove with tongs and drain on paper towels. As soon as the tubes are cool enough to handle, slide them out and leave the pastries on a rack to cool.

To make the filling, mash the ricotta with a fork. Blend in the sugar and vanilla extract, then mix in the lemon zest, candied peel, glacé cherries and chocolate. Fill the pastries, either with a piping bag or a spoon. Arrange on a plate and dust with icing sugar for serving. The cannoli should be eaten soon after they are filled.

café life... The Italian café can seem functional and sparse—and in many ways it is—for here coffee, topped with whirled cream or vanilla sugar, is not something to be sipped and gossiped over. Instead, an espresso is as workmanlike as the beautiful metal coffee machine, the *gaggia*, which steams away in every café, its long lever pulled down to force out the trickle of dark brown coffee.

Many Italians begin their day standing up in their local bar—a multi-purpose establishment that can provide a shot of grappa or a panini, as well as coffee. Knocking back cappuccinos and tucking into a breakfast *cornetto,* a custard or jam-filled croissant, the customers are usually in and out in 10 minutes. Just enough time to glance at a paper's football news and have a quick conversation with the *barista,* the coffee-maker, in a fog of espresso aroma before heading out into the morning sunshine.

By mid-morning, many of these people have already returned for an espresso—downed like a shot—on the run between meetings or errands. These tiny, jolting cups are an essential part of the Italian working day and often it is in a busy airport or train station where you see the café experience pared back to its most minimalist. A plain metal counter, stacks of white or dark brown china cups and the *gaggia.* Here the choice is between an espresso, called simply *caffé,* dramatic and intense with its head of foamy *crema,* or a cappuccino, the same espresso topped with spoonfuls of frothy steamed milk. With such simplicity, the quality of the coffee itself is everything.

Only in the cities has the café experience evolved into more than daily sustenance. Many have a *Gran Caffé,* where a coffee can be enjoyed in a more refined style. Here there are menus and waiters, and coffee is served in elegant glasses. Trieste is Italy's coffee port, for coffee is of course not native at all to this country, and it has many such cafés. Venice, where coffee entered Europe in the sixteenth century, has some of the grandest cafes in its St Mark's square where coffee, art and politics first formed their heady mix.

300 g (10½ oz) Madeira or pound cake
3 tablespoons maraschino liqueur
3 tablespoons brandy
500 ml (2 cups) thick (double) cream
90 g (¾ cup) icing (confectioners') sugar
150 g (5½ oz) dark chocolate, roughly chopped
50 g (1¾ oz) blanched almonds
25 g (1 oz) skinned hazelnuts
25 g (1 oz) candied peel, chopped
cocoa powder, to dust
icing (confectioners') sugar, to dust

Serves 6

Cut the cake into 1 cm (½ inch) slices and then cut each slice into two triangles. Combine the maraschino and brandy and sprinkle them over the cake.

Line a round 1.5 litre (6-cup) bowl with a layer of plastic wrap and then with the cake slices. Arrange the slices with the narrow point of each triangle pointing into the bottom of the bowl to form a star pattern, fitting each piece snugly against the others so you don't have any gaps. Cut smaller triangles to fit the gaps along the top and keep the rest of the cake for the top.

Whip the cream until soft peaks form and then whisk in the icing sugar until you have a stiff mixture. Add about a third of the chocolate and the almonds, hazelnuts and candied peel. Mix together thoroughly, then fill the cake-lined bowl with half the mixture, making a hollow in the middle and drawing the mixture up the sides. Leave in the fridge.

Melt the rest of the chocolate in a heatproof bowl over a saucepan of simmering water, or in a microwave. Fold it into the remaining cream mixture. Spoon this into the bowl and then cover the top with a layer of cake triangles, leaving no gaps. Cover the bowl with plastic wrap and refrigerate overnight.

To serve, unmould the zuccotto and use a triangular piece of cardboard as a template to dust the top with alternating segments of cocoa and icing sugar.

zuccotto

amaretti

125 g (4½ oz) blanched almonds
125 g (1 cup) icing (confectioners') sugar
3 teaspoons plain (all-purpose) flour
2 egg whites
80 g (⅓ cup) caster (superfine) sugar
1 teaspoon almond extract

Makes 15

Preheat the oven to 180°C (350°F/Gas 4). Put the almonds, icing sugar and flour in a mortar and pestle or food processor and grind to a fine powder (be careful not to overwork the mixture or it will become oily).

Whisk the egg whites in a clean dry glass bowl until soft peaks form. Add the caster sugar a tablespoon at a time and beat continuously until you have a stiff shiny mixture. Fold in the almond mixture and the almond extract until just blended.

Spoon the mixture into a piping bag with a 1 cm (½ inch) plain nozzle and pipe 3 cm (1¼ inch) wide mounds, well spaced, onto a baking tray. Smooth the top of each biscuit with a damp finger and bake for 40 minutes until they are light brown. Turn off the oven, leave the door ajar and let the biscuits cool and dry out. Store in an airtight container.

basics

tapenade

250 g (9 oz) whole black olives, pitted
50 g (1¾ oz) tin anchovy fillets
1 tablespoon capers, drained
2 garlic cloves, crushed
15 g (½ oz) basil, finely chopped
grated zest and juice of 1 lemon
185 ml (¾ cup) extra virgin olive oil

Finely chop the olives, anchovies and capers together with a knife or food processor and place in a bowl. Add the garlic, basil, lemon zest and juice, stir in the olive oil and season well. The tapenade will keep in an airtight container in the fridge for up to a month. Makes 375 g (1½ cups).

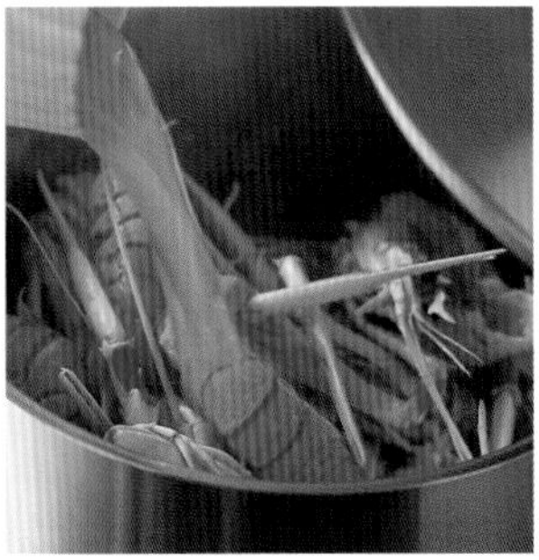

fish stock

500 g (1 lb 2 oz) fish bones
12 prawn shells
1 small onion, roughly chopped
1 carrot, roughly chopped
15 g (¼ cup) roughly chopped parsley, stalks reserved

Rinse the fish bones in cold water, removing any blood or intestines. Put the fish bones and prawn shells in a large saucepan with just enough water to cover. Bring slowly to a simmer, skimming any froth from the surface. Add the onion, carrot and the stalks from the parsley, then simmer gently for 20 minutes. Strain through a fine colander and measure 1.5 litres (6 cups) stock. If there is less than this, add a little water; if there is more than this, put the strained stock back into the saucepan and simmer until reduced to 1.5 litres (6 cups).

béchamel sauce

65 g (2¼ oz) butter
40 g (1½ oz) plain (all-purpose) flour
pinch of grated nutmeg
625 ml (2½ cups) milk
1 bay leaf

Heat the butter in a saucepan over low heat. Add the flour and nutmeg and cook, stirring, for 1 minute. Remove from the heat and gradually stir in the milk. Add the bay leaf, return to the heat and simmer, stirring often, until the sauce thickens. Season, cover with plastic wrap to prevent a skin forming, and cool. Discard the bay leaf. Makes 750 ml (3 cups).

tomato sauce

120 g (4 oz) plum (Roma) tomatoes
3 basil leaves
2 garlic cloves, crushed
1 tablespoon tomato passata
2 teaspoons extra virgin olive oil

Core the tomatoes and purée in a food processor with the basil leaves (or chop the tomatoes and basil very finely and stir together). Stir in the garlic, passata and olive oil and season well. Leave for at least 30 minutes before serving to allow the flavours to blend. Use on pizzas, toss through pasta or serve with arancini or suppli. Makes 185 ml (¾ cup).

pesto

2 garlic cloves
50 g (⅓ cup) pine nuts
80 g (1⅔ cups) basil leaves
4 tablespoons grated Parmesan
150 ml (5 fl oz) extra virgin olive oil

Put the garlic, pine nuts, basil and Parmesan in a mortar and pestle or a food processor and pound or mix to a paste. Add the oil in a steady stream, mixing continuously. Add salt if necessary. Refrigerate in a sterilized jar, covered with a layer of olive oil, for up to 3 weeks. Makes 185 ml (¾ cup).

glossary

al dente Meaning 'to the tooth'. Pasta and risotto rice are cooked until they are *al dente*—the outside is tender but the centre still has a little resistance or 'bite'. Pasta cooked beyond this point becomes soggy.

artichoke ***(carciofo)*** The edible flower of a member of the thistle family. Some have thorns and the types vary greatly in size. The largest are usually boiled, but the smallest and most tender can be eaten raw as antipasto. Most common varieties include Romanesco (large and purple), Precoce di Chioggia (large and green), Violetto Toscano (small and tender enough to eat raw) and Spinoso di Palermo (a purple variety from Sicily).

bresaola Lean beef that is cured and air-dried for 2–3 months—a speciality of the Valtellina Valley in Lombardia. Has a dark red colour and stronger flavour than prosciutto. Serve thinly sliced.

cannellini beans These are white, kidney-shaped beans, also known as Italian haricot beans or white kidney beans. Available fresh, dried or tinned.

caperberries The fruit of the caper bush, which appear after the flowers. They are usually preserved in brine and served as an accompaniment, like olives.

capers The pickled flowers of the caper bush. Available preserved in brine, vinegar or salt and should be rinsed well and squeezed dry before use.

casalinga Means 'home-made' or 'homely'. When attributed to sausages or salami, it generally means having a coarse texture and earthy flavour.

cavolo nero Cabbage with long, dark green leaves which appear to be almost black. Used mainly in Tuscan cooking. Savoy cabbage can be substituted.

cetriolini Small gherkins. If unavailable, use cornichons or small cocktail gherkins.

ciabatta Slipper-shaped Italian bread with a rough, open texture. Made from a very wet dough, which allows large bubbles to form and gives a thin crust, ciabatta quickly goes stale and is best eaten on the day it is bought or made.

cipolline Small white onions, usually flattened in appearance.

coppa A cured pork made from half pork fat and half pig's neck and shoulder. It is rolled and cured in a casing and, when sliced, resembles a fatty sausage.

cornmeal See *polenta*.

country-style bread Any bread that is bought as a whole loaf and has a rough texture. Pugliese, ciabatta and pane Toscano are all examples. Other white bread is not a suitable substitute.

croccante Caramelized nuts, usually almonds but sometimes hazelnuts (these are also known as pralines).

finocchiona A type of salami from Tuscany, flavoured with wild fennel seeds. The salami is very often large and is aged for up to a year before use. It also comes in a more crumbly version called sbriciolona.

flat-leaf parsley Also known as Italian or continental parsley. Used as an ingredient rather than a garnish, unlike curly parsley.

fontina A traditional mountain cheese from the Valle d'Aosta in Piemonte. Full-fat and semi-soft with a sweetish flavour, fontina melts evenly and well and so is particularly good for cooking.

Gorgonzola A blue cheese, originally made in Gorgonzola in Lombardia but now produced in other regions as well. It melts well and is often used in sauces. If not available, use another full-fat blue cheese.

juniper berries Blackish-purple berries with a resin flavour. Used in stews and game dishes. Crush the berries slightly before use to release their flavour.

Marsala A fortified wine from Marsala in Sicily that comes in varying degrees of dryness and sweetness. Dry Marsalas are used in savoury dishes, and sweet ones in desserts such as zabaione. Don't use sweet Marsala in savoury dishes.

mascarpone A cream cheese originally from Lombardia. Made with cream rather than milk, it is very high in fat. Generally used in desserts such as tiramisu, or instead of cream in sauces.

misticanza A Roman salad that was once made of wild greens. Today it is generally a mixture of rocket (arugula), purslane, sorrel, mint, dandelion, wild fennel and endive with some lettuce. In Umbria it also refers to a mixture of dried beans used for soups.

mozzarella Originally, all mozzarella in Italy was made from the prized milk of water buffaloes, which gives a creamy, fragrant fresh cheese. Most mozzarella is now made with cow's milk, with the resulting texture and taste being slightly different. Buffalo milk mozzarella is available in some places.

olive Eating olives can be named after the region they come from, such as Ligurian; their curing style, such as Sicilian; or their variety, such as Cerignola. Though green and black olives have a different flavour, they can be used interchangeably in recipes unless the final colour is a factor.

olive oil Extra virgin and virgin olive oils are pressed without any heat or chemicals and are best used in simple uncooked dishes and for salads. Pure olive oil can be used for cooking or deep-frying. Different varieties of olives are grown all over Italy and the oil of each region has a distinctive taste. Tuscan oil tends to be full-bodied and peppery; Ligurian oil pale and subtle; and Pugliese and Sicilian oil fruity and sharp.

pancetta Cured belly of pork, somewhat like streaky bacon. Available in flat pieces or rolled up (*arrotolata*), and both smoked and unsmoked. Generally used, sliced or cut into cubes, as an ingredient in dishes like spaghetti carbonara.

passata Meaning 'puréed', this most commonly refers to a smooth uncooked tomato pulp bought in tins or jars. It is best to buy passata without added herbs and flavourings.

pecorino One of Italy's most popular cheeses, with virtually every region producing its own version. Made from sheep's milk and always by the same method, although the result varies according to the milk and ageing process used. Pecorino Romano is a well-known hard variety from Lazio and Sardinia.

peperoncini The Italian name for chillies, these are popular in the cooking of the South, and are also served there as a condiment. The smallest are called *diavolilli*.

polenta The name of the dish and also the ingredient itself, which is ground corn. The cornmeal comes in different grades of coarseness. Finer varieties are better in cakes and coarse ones to accompany stews. A white cornmeal is also available.

porcini The Italian name for a cep or boletus mushroom. Usually bought dried and reconstituted by soaking in boiling water, but available fresh in the spring and autumn.

prosciutto Italian name for ham. *Prosciutto crudo* is cured ham and includes Parma ham and San Daniele. *Prosciutto cotto* is cooked ham.

radicchio A salad leaf of the chicory family with slightly bitter red leaves. There are several varieties: radicchio di Castelfranco, di Chioggia and rosso di Verona are similar to a red cabbage with round leaves; radicchio di Treviso has longer, pointed leaves.

risotto rice Round-grained, very absorbent rice, cultivated in northern Italy. Risotto rice comes in four categories, classified not by quality but by the size of each grain. The smallest, Riso Comune (common rice) is very quick to cook (12–13 minutes), and is ideal for rice pudding. Semifino rice includes varieties like vialone nano and cooks in about 15 minutes. Fino takes a minute longer and has more bite. The largest, Superfino, includes arborio and carnaroli and takes about 20 minutes.

soffritto The flavour base for many soups, stews and risottos. Soffritto is a mixture of fried ingredients like onion, celery, carrot, garlic, pancetta and herbs. It means literally to 'under-fry' and the mixture should be sweated rather than coloured.

squid/cuttlefish ink Used to colour and flavour pasta and risotto. The ink is stored in a sac that can be removed from whole squid and cuttlefish or bought in sachets from fishmongers or delicatessens.

Taleggio A mountain cheese originally from the Italian Alps near Bergamo, but now also made in other regions. Taleggio is a very good table and cooking cheese and should be eaten young—its flavour becomes more acidic with age. It is made in squares and has a pink-yellow crust and creamy centre.

truffles Both black and white truffles can be found in Italy. The black ones come from Umbria (especially around Norcia), Piemonte and Emilia-Romagna. The white ones come from Alba (considered the best), Emilia-Romagna, Le Marche, Tuscany and Umbria. Fresh truffles are very expensive but only a tiny amount is needed. Preserved truffles are also available, as is truffle oil.

index

Published by Murdoch Books®, a division of Murdoch Magazines Pty. Ltd.
 First published 2003. Reprinted 2003.

Chief Executive: Juliet Rogers

Publisher: Kay Scarlett

Creative Director: Marylouise Brammer
Design Concept: Vivien Valk
Designer: Susanne Geppert
Food Editor: Lulu Grimes
Stylist: Mary Harris
Stylist's Assistant: Briget Palmer
Editorial Director: Diana Hill
Editor: Wendy Stephen

National Library of Australia Cataloguing-in-Publication Data
A little taste of Italy. Includes index.
ISBN 0 86411 947 X.
1. Cookery, Italian. 641.5945

PRINTED IN CHINA by Leefung-Asco

Murdoch Books® Australia
GPO Box 1203, Sydney, NSW 1045
Phone: 61 (0) 2 4352 7000
Fax: 61 (0) 2 4352 7026

Murdoch Books® UK
Erico House
6th Floor North
93-99 Upper Richmond Road
London SW15 2TG
Phone: +44 (0) 20 8355 1480
Fax: +44 (0) 20 8355 1499

IMPORTANT: Those who might be at risk from the effects of salmonella food poisoning (the elderly, pregnant women, young children and those suffering from immune deficiency diseases) should consult their GP with any concerns about eating raw eggs.